Mastering YouTube Algorithms

A GUIDE TO BOOST YOUR VIEWS

Introduction

The Power of YouTube

YouTube has emerged as one of the most influential platforms in the digital age, offering immense opportunities for content creators, businesses, educators, and consumers. With over 2 billion logged-in monthly users, it boasts global reach and accessibility, being available in more than 100 countries and supporting 80 languages. This vast reach allows creators to connect with diverse audiences worldwide, expanding their influence far beyond geographical boundaries.

The platform hosts an extensive range of content, from tutorials and educational videos to entertainment and vlogs, catering to various interests and preferences. This diversity not only attracts a wide audience but also enables creators to build a loyal community and foster deeper viewer engagement. The ability to monetize content through ad revenue, channel memberships, and other means makes YouTube an attractive platform for aspiring creators and businesses looking to diversify their income streams.

The platform's influence extends beyond entertainment; YouTube influencers have the power to shape opinions, trends, and behaviors.

They can advocate for social causes, raise awareness on important issues, and inspire positive change, making YouTube a critical space for social impact and advocacy. Additionally, YouTube encourages creativity and innovation, allowing individuals to express themselves and experiment with different formats and styles, pushing the boundaries of traditional media.

YouTube also provides robust analytics tools that offer insights into viewer behavior, demographics, and engagement metrics. Understanding this data is key to optimizing content strategy and improving overall performance. Furthermore, the platform fosters a sense of community among creators and viewers, offering numerous collaboration and networking opportunities that can lead to increased exposure and new opportunities.

The power of YouTube continues to grow as the platform evolves and introduces new features. With advancements in technology, such as virtual reality and artificial intelligence, the potential for innovative content and enhanced viewer experiences is limitless. By understanding and leveraging these aspects, creators and businesses can unlock the full potential of YouTube and achieve long-term success on this dynamic platform.

Why Understanding the Algorithm Matters

Understanding the YouTube algorithm is crucial for anyone looking to succeed on the platform, whether you're a content creator, marketer, or business owner. The algorithm determines which videos are recommended to users, which can significantly impact your channel's visibility, engagement, and growth. Here's why a deep understanding of the YouTube algorithm is essential:

1. Increased Visibility
The YouTube algorithm plays a pivotal role in determining which videos are promoted on the platform. By understanding how the algorithm works, you can optimize your content to increase the likelihood of it being recommended to viewers. This means more exposure and a greater chance of reaching a wider audience. Without this knowledge, your videos might get lost in the vast sea of content available on YouTube.

2. Higher Engagement Rates
Videos that align well with the algorithm's criteria are more likely to be shown to users who are interested in that content, leading to higher engagement rates. This includes likes, comments, shares, and watch time.

Understanding what the algorithm prioritizes, such as viewer retention and interaction, allows you to create content that keeps viewers engaged and encourages them to interact with your channel.

3. Improved Content Strategy

A solid grasp of the algorithm helps in refining your content strategy. You can focus on creating videos that are not only high-quality but also algorithm-friendly. This involves using appropriate keywords, compelling thumbnails, and engaging titles. By aligning your content with what the algorithm favors, you can systematically grow your channel and ensure consistent performance over time.

4. Audience Growth

The algorithm is designed to keep viewers on the platform by recommending content that matches their interests. By tailoring your content to these preferences, you can attract new subscribers and retain existing ones. Understanding the algorithm helps you create videos that meet the needs and desires of your target audience, fostering steady growth in your subscriber base.

5. Monetization Opportunities

Greater visibility and engagement directly translate to better monetization opportunities. YouTube's Partner Program and other monetization options rely heavily on your channel's performance, which is influenced by the algorithm.

By optimizing your content to meet algorithmic standards, you can increase your earnings from ads, sponsorships, and other revenue streams available on the platform.

6. Competitive Advantage
In a crowded digital landscape, understanding the YouTube algorithm gives you a competitive edge. Many creators may not invest the time to learn about the algorithm, giving those who do a significant advantage. This knowledge allows you to outperform competitors who are less informed about how to optimize their content for better visibility and engagement.

7. Adaptation to Changes
The YouTube algorithm is not static; it evolves to improve user experience and adapt to changing viewer behaviors. By staying informed about these changes, you can quickly adjust your content strategy to maintain or enhance your channel's performance. Creators who understand and adapt to algorithm updates can continue to thrive, even as the platform evolves.

8. Optimizing Viewer Retention
Viewer retention is a critical factor in the algorithm's decision-making process. Videos that keep viewers watching for longer periods are favored.

By understanding this aspect of the algorithm, you can create content that holds viewers' attention, such as by structuring your videos with engaging introductions, maintaining a steady pace, and delivering value throughout.

9. Targeted Recommendations

The algorithm uses complex data points to recommend videos to specific user segments. By understanding how these recommendations work, you can better tailor your content to fit niche markets and specific viewer interests. This targeted approach helps you build a dedicated and engaged audience that is more likely to interact with your content and support your channel.

10. Enhancing Viewer Experience

Ultimately, the goal of the algorithm is to enhance the viewer experience by providing relevant and engaging content. By aligning your content creation process with this goal, you not only benefit from increased visibility but also contribute to a positive viewer experience. This fosters loyalty and encourages viewers to return to your channel for more content.

In conclusion, understanding the YouTube algorithm is essential for maximizing your channel's potential. It helps you increase visibility, boost engagement rates, refine your content strategy, grow your audience, and seize monetization opportunities.

Additionally, it provides a competitive edge, aids in adapting to changes, and allows for targeted recommendations and optimized viewer retention. By leveraging this knowledge, you can enhance the overall viewer experience and achieve sustained success on the platform.

To summarize, understanding your audience's preferences and behavior is paramount. It enables you to create content that resonates with viewers, making them more likely to engage with and share your videos.

This deeper connection with your audience fosters loyalty and encourages repeat viewership. Furthermore, the insights gained from analyzing viewer data can help you identify trends and adapt your content strategy accordingly, ensuring that you stay relevant in a constantly evolving digital landscape.

In essence, a data-driven approach to content creation not only improves the quality of your videos but also ensures that you are meeting the needs and expectations of your audience. This, in turn, leads to higher viewer satisfaction, better engagement metrics, and a stronger presence on the platform. By continuously refining your content based on audience insights, you can build a sustainable and thriving channel that stands out in the competitive world of online video.

Chapter 1
Getting Started with YouTube

Setting Up Your Channel

Setting up your YouTube channel correctly from the beginning is essential for creating a strong foundation for your success. This involves several key steps, from choosing the right name and branding to optimizing your channel's settings and layout. Here's a comprehensive guide to setting up your YouTube channel:

1. Creating a Google Account

To start a YouTube channel, you need a Google account. If you don't already have one, go to the Google sign-up page and create an account. If you have a Google account, you can use it to sign in to YouTube.

2. Channel Name and Branding

Your channel name and branding are critical elements that represent your identity on YouTube. Choose a name that is unique, memorable, and reflective of your content. Ensure it is easy to spell and pronounce. Once you've settled on a name, create a cohesive brand identity, including a logo and banner image.

- **Channel Name:** Make it relevant to your content and easy to remember.

- **Logo:** Design a simple and recognizable logo that looks good in small sizes.
- **Banner Image:** Create a visually appealing banner that communicates your channel's theme or value proposition.

3. Channel Description and Keywords

Your channel description is your opportunity to tell potential subscribers what your channel is about. Write a clear and concise description that outlines the type of content you produce and what viewers can expect. Incorporate relevant keywords to improve searchability.

- **Description:** Highlight your channel's purpose, the value you provide, and your upload schedule.
- **Keywords:** Use keywords that describe your niche and content to help YouTube's algorithm understand and promote your channel.

4. Customizing Your Channel Layout

Customize your channel layout to make it user-friendly and visually appealing. This includes organizing your videos into sections and playlists, setting a featured video for new visitors, and customizing the channel homepage.

- **Sections:** Group related videos into sections to help viewers find content easily.

- **Playlists:** Create playlists to organize your videos by theme or series.
- **Featured Video:** Select a video that introduces your channel to new visitors or highlights your best content.

5. Setting Up Channel Art

Channel art includes your profile picture and banner image. Ensure these visuals are high quality and reflect your brand's identity.

- **Profile Picture:** Use a high-resolution image, typically your logo or a professional headshot.
- **Banner Image:** The banner should be **2560 x 1440** pixels to ensure it looks good on all devices. Include text or graphics that represent your channel's theme.

7. Creating a Channel Trailer

A channel trailer is a short video that introduces new visitors to your content. It should be engaging and provide a clear overview of what your channel offers.

- **Length:** Keep it under one minute to maintain viewer interest.
- **Content:** Highlight your best content, your upload schedule, and what viewers can expect from your channel.

- **Call to Action:** Encourage viewers to subscribe to your channel.

8. Setting Up Channel Settings

Optimize your channel settings to ensure your content is discoverable and meets YouTube's guidelines.

- **Privacy Settings:** Decide whether to keep your subscriptions and saved playlists private or public.
- **Default Upload Settings:** Set default titles, descriptions, tags, and privacy settings for your uploads to save time.
- **Moderation Settings:** Enable comment moderation to manage viewer interactions and maintain a positive community.

9. Adding Keywords and Tags

Keywords and tags are crucial for SEO and helping the YouTube algorithm understand your content. Add relevant keywords to your channel's settings and use specific tags for each video to improve discoverability.

- **Channel Keywords:** Include broad terms related to your content niche.
- **Video Tags:** Use specific and relevant tags for each video to enhance searchability. These tags should directly relate to the content of the individual video and help viewers find your video when they search for related topics.

10. Creating a Content Plan

Develop a content plan to ensure you have a consistent upload schedule and a clear direction for your channel. Plan your content around topics that resonate with your target audience.

- **Content Calendar:** Schedule your video uploads to maintain consistency.
- **Content Ideas:** Brainstorm topics and series that align with your channel's theme.
- **Production Schedule:** Allocate time for filming, editing, and uploading to stay on track.

11. Understanding YouTube Policies

Familiarize yourself with YouTube's community guidelines and policies to avoid potential issues. Ensure your content complies with YouTube's rules to prevent strikes or bans.

- **Community Guidelines:** Understand YouTube's rules regarding content, copyright, and monetization.
- **Content Policies:** Stay informed about what content is allowed and what could lead to penalties. YouTube has specific policies regarding various types of content, such as misinformation, inappropriate content, and copyright violations. Regularly review these policies to ensure your content does not inadvertently breach any rules. Understanding these guidelines will help you maintain a good standing with the platform and avoid demonetization or removal of your videos.

12. Promoting Your Channel

Once your channel is set up, start promoting it to build your audience. Utilize social media, collaborations, and SEO to increase your channel's visibility.

- **Social Media Promotion:** Share your videos on your social media profiles to reach a broader audience.
- **Collaborations:** Partner with other YouTubers to cross-promote content and attract new subscribers.
- **SEO:** Optimize your video titles, descriptions, and tags to improve search rankings.

By following these steps, you can set up a YouTube channel that is visually appealing, user-friendly, and optimized for growth. A well-structured channel not only attracts viewers but also encourages them to subscribe and engage with your content, laying the groundwork for long-term success on the platform.

Customizing your channel is essential. Start with designing a visually appealing banner that reflects your brand and is properly sized for different devices. Use a clear and recognizable profile picture, such as your logo or a professional photo. Creating a compelling channel trailer can introduce new visitors to your content and encourage them to subscribe.

Defining Your Niche and Target Audience

Defining your niche and target audience is a critical step in establishing a successful YouTube channel. By identifying a specific niche and understanding the audience you want to reach, you can create content that resonates deeply with viewers, fosters engagement, and builds a loyal following. Here's a comprehensive guide to help you define your niche and target audience:

1. Understanding the Importance of a Niche

A niche is a specific segment of a broader market that you focus on with your content. It's crucial because it allows you to stand out in the crowded YouTube landscape. Here's why defining a niche is important:

- **Specialization:** Specializing in a particular area helps you become an authority in that field. Viewers seeking content in your niche are more likely to find and trust your channel.
- **Audience Loyalty:** A well-defined niche attracts a dedicated audience who are interested in your specific content. This loyalty can lead to higher engagement and retention rates.
- **Content Focus:** Knowing your niche allows you to create focused, relevant content that addresses the interests and needs of your audience, making your channel more appealing and cohesive.

2. Identifying Your Passion and Expertise

Start by identifying your passion and expertise, as these will sustain your interest and credibility in the long run. Consider the following:

- **Interests:** What topics are you passionate about? Your enthusiasm will translate into engaging content.
- **Skills and Knowledge:** What are you knowledgeable about? Leveraging your expertise can help establish you as a trusted source in your niche.
- **Sustainability:** Can you consistently produce content on this topic? Ensure there's enough scope for ongoing content creation.

3. Researching Potential Niches

Conduct thorough research to find potential niches that align with your interests and have a viable audience. Here's how:

- **Keyword Research:** Use tools like Google Trends, YouTube's search bar, and keyword planners to find popular search terms related to your interests.
- **Competitor Analysis:** Look at other channels in potential niches. Analyze their content, engagement, and growth to identify gaps you can fill or ways to differentiate yourself.
- **Audience Demand:** Assess the demand for content in each niche. Are there active communities, forums, or social media groups discussing these topics?

4. Evaluating Niche Viability

Once you have a list of potential niches, evaluate their viability based on these factors:

- **Audience Size:** Is there a substantial audience interested in this niche? While a larger audience can mean more competition, it also offers more potential viewers.
- **Monetization Potential:** Can you monetize content in this niche? Consider ad revenue, sponsorships, merchandise, and other income streams.
- **Content Longevity:** Is this a trending topic or a timeless subject? Ensure there's potential for long-term content creation.

5. Defining Your Target Audience

Your target audience consists of the specific group of people you want to reach with your content. Defining this group helps tailor your content to their preferences and needs. Here's how to identify your target audience:

- **Demographics:** Consider age, gender, location, language, education level, and occupation. This basic information helps create a general profile of your audience.
- **Psychographics:** Understand your audience's interests, values, lifestyle, and personality. These insights help create content that resonates on a deeper level.

- **Behavioral Insights:** Analyze your audience's behavior, including their viewing habits, content preferences, and online activities. Tools like YouTube Analytics and social media insights can provide valuable data.

6. Creating Audience Personas

Audience personas are fictional representations of your ideal viewers based on demographic, psychographic, and behavioral data. They help you visualize and understand your audience better. Here's how to create them:

- **Persona Details:** Give each persona a name, age, occupation, and background. Include interests, goals, challenges, and preferred content types.
- **Use Cases:** Describe how each persona interacts with your content. What problems do they seek to solve? What motivates them to subscribe and engage with your channel?

7. Aligning Content with Audience Needs

Tailor your content to meet the specific needs and interests of your target audience. Consider the following:

- **Value Proposition:** Clearly define the value your content provides. Whether it's entertainment, education, inspiration, or practical advice, ensure it aligns with your audience's needs.

- **Content Formats:** Choose formats that resonate with your audience, such as tutorials, reviews, vlogs, interviews, or storytelling. Experiment with different styles to see what works best.
- **Engagement Strategies:** Develop strategies to engage your audience, such as asking questions, encouraging comments, and creating interactive content like polls and live streams.

8. Testing and Refining Your Approach

Defining your niche and target audience is an ongoing process. Continuously test and refine your approach based on feedback and performance metrics:

- **Analytics:** Regularly review YouTube Analytics to understand how your content is performing. Look at metrics like watch time, audience retention, and engagement rates.
- **Feedback:** Pay attention to viewer comments, messages, and social media interactions. Use this feedback to improve your content and better meet audience expectations.
- **Adaptation:** Be willing to adapt your content strategy based on what you learn. Experiment with new ideas, formats, and topics to see how your audience responds.

By defining your niche and target audience, you lay the foundation for a focused, engaging, and successful YouTube channel. This clarity helps you create content that resonates deeply with viewers, builds a loyal community, and sets you apart in the crowded YouTube landscape.

Identifying your passion and expertise ensures that your content is both enjoyable to create and valuable to your audience. Thorough research into your audience's demographics, interests, and pain points, coupled with competitor analysis, allows you to understand what works and where you can differentiate yourself. Finally, defining your unique selling proposition (USP) will solidify your channel's identity and appeal, making it easier to attract and retain loyal viewers.

A well-defined niche allows you to streamline your content strategy and stay consistent with your uploads. Consistency is key on YouTube, as it helps build anticipation and reliability among your viewers. When your audience knows what to expect from your channel, they are more likely to return for more content and engage with it. Additionally, a focused niche makes it easier for you to brainstorm content ideas, as you have clear boundaries and themes to explore. This not only saves time but also ensures that each video you produce is relevant and valuable to your target audience.

Understanding YouTube's Community Guidelines

YouTube's Community Guidelines are essential for maintaining a safe and positive environment for users. Adhering to these guidelines is crucial for the success and longevity of your channel. Violating these rules can lead to content removal, channel strikes, and even account termination. Here's an in-depth look at YouTube's Community Guidelines and how to ensure your content complies with them:

1. Overview of Community Guidelines

YouTube's Community Guidelines are a set of rules designed to ensure the platform remains a safe, respectful, and engaging place for everyone. These guidelines cover various aspects of content creation and behavior, including the type of content allowed, user conduct, and the handling of sensitive information. Key areas covered include:

- **Nudity and Sexual Content**
- **Harmful or Dangerous Content**
- **Hate Speech**
- **Harassment and Cyberbullying**
- **Spam, Deceptive Practices, and Scams**
- **Violent or Graphic Content**
- **Child Safety**
- **Copyright Infringement**

2. Nudity and Sexual Content

YouTube restricts content that contains nudity, pornography, or sexually explicit material. This includes:

- **Explicit Content:** Videos that depict sexual acts, nudity, or graphic sexual content.
- **Sexualization of Minors:** Any content that sexualizes minors is strictly prohibited.
- **Non-consensual Content:** Videos that involve sexual harassment, exploitation, or non-consensual sexual activities.
-

To ensure compliance, avoid uploading or sharing any content that might be deemed sexually explicit or inappropriate for all age groups.

3. Harmful or Dangerous Content

YouTube prohibits content that promotes or glorifies harmful or dangerous activities. This includes:

- **Self-Harm:** Content that promotes self-harm, suicide, or eating disorders.
- **Dangerous Challenges:** Videos that encourage dangerous activities or challenges that could result in injury.
- **Drug Use:** Content that promotes the use of illegal drugs or the abuse of legal substances.

Ensure that your content does not encourage viewers to engage in harmful or risky behavior.

4. Hate Speech

YouTube does not allow content that promotes hatred against individuals or groups based on attributes such as race, ethnicity, religion, disability, gender, age, nationality, veteran status, sexual orientation, or gender identity. This includes:

- **Derogatory Language:** Using slurs or derogatory terms to describe individuals or groups.
- **Incitement to Violence:** Content that incites violence against individuals or groups based on their attributes.
- **Dehumanizing Speech:** Videos that dehumanize individuals or groups by comparing them to animals, insects, pests, etc.

To comply, avoid making any discriminatory or hateful remarks in your videos.

5. Harassment and Cyberbullying

YouTube aims to protect users from harassment and cyberbullying. This includes:

- **Targeted Harassment:** Videos that single out individuals for abuse or humiliation.
- **Threats:** Content that includes threats of physical harm, stalking, or harassment.
- **Invasion of Privacy:** Sharing personal information or images of individuals without their consent.

Create a respectful and supportive environment by refraining from targeting or harassing individuals in your content.

6. Spam, Deceptive Practices, and Scams

YouTube has strict rules against spam, deceptive practices, and scams. This includes:

- **Misleading Metadata:** Using misleading titles, descriptions, or tags to attract viewers.
- **Scams:** Content that promises false rewards, giveaways, or financial schemes.
- **Repetitive Comments:** Posting large amounts of repetitive comments or links.

Ensure your content and metadata are accurate and not designed to deceive viewers.

7. Violent or Graphic Content

Content that is excessively violent or graphic is prohibited on YouTube. This includes:

- **Real Violence:** Videos showing real-life violence, including fights, assaults, or accidents.
- **Disturbing Content:** Content that is intended to shock or disgust viewers.
- **Animal Cruelty:** Videos depicting cruelty towards animals.

Avoid uploading content that could be considered excessively violent or disturbing.

8. Child Safety

YouTube places a high priority on protecting children. This includes:

- **Exploitation:** Content that exploits or endangers children, such as child abuse or exploitation.
- **Inappropriate Content for Minors:** Videos with mature themes that are not suitable for children.
- **Privacy Violations:** Sharing personal information about children without consent.

Ensure your content is appropriate for all audiences and does not exploit or endanger minors.

9. Copyright Infringement

YouTube takes copyright infringement seriously and protects the rights of content creators. This includes:

- **Using Copyrighted Material:** Uploading videos that contain copyrighted music, videos, images, or other content without permission.
- **Fair Use Misinterpretation:** Misusing the fair use doctrine to justify unauthorized use of copyrighted material.
- **Repeated Infringement:** Consistently violating copyright rules can lead to account termination.

To avoid copyright issues, use your own original content or obtain proper licenses for any third-party material you include in your videos.

10. Ensuring Compliance

To ensure your content complies with YouTube's Community Guidelines, follow these best practices:

- **Review Guidelines:** Regularly review YouTube's Community Guidelines to stay updated on any changes or new policies.
- **Self-Audit:** Before uploading, audit your content to ensure it meets all guidelines and does not contain any prohibited material.
- **Educate Yourself:** Take advantage of YouTube's resources, such as the Creator Academy, to learn more about the guidelines and best practices.
- **Seek Feedback:** If you're unsure about the compliance of your content, seek feedback from peers or community members.

11. Handling Violations

If YouTube determines that your content violates its Community Guidelines, it may remove the content and issue a strike against your channel. Here's how to handle violations:

- **Understand Strikes:** Learn about YouTube's strike system. The first strike usually serves as a warning, but subsequent strikes can lead to more severe consequences, including temporary bans or permanent removal.

- **Appeal Process:** If you believe a strike was issued in error, use the appeal process to have YouTube review the decision.
- **Corrective Action:** Remove or modify any content that violates guidelines to avoid further strikes and ensure future compliance.

Understanding and adhering to YouTube's Community Guidelines is essential for maintaining a positive, compliant, and successful channel. By creating content that respects these rules, you can build a trustworthy and engaging presence on the platform, ensuring long-term success and a strong connection with your audience.

Violating these guidelines can result in penalties, including video removals, demonetization, or even channel termination. Therefore, staying informed about the latest updates to these policies is crucial. This includes avoiding content that promotes hate speech, violence, misinformation, or other harmful behaviors. By aligning your content with YouTube's standards, you protect your channel from potential risks and demonstrate a commitment to ethical and responsible content creation.

Moreover, adhering to Community Guidelines fosters a safe and inclusive environment for your audience. Viewers are more likely to engage with and support channels that prioritize respectful and constructive interactions.

Chapter 2
The Basics of the YouTube Algorithm

History and Evolution of the YouTube Algorithm

Understanding the history and evolution of the YouTube algorithm provides crucial insights into how the platform has grown and adapted to meet the needs of its users. Over the years, YouTube's algorithm has undergone significant changes to improve user experience, optimize content discovery, and enhance viewer engagement. Here's an in-depth look at the key phases of the YouTube algorithm's evolution:

1. The Early Days: 2005-2011

When YouTube was launched in 2005, its initial algorithm was relatively simple, focusing primarily on the number of views a video received. The more views a video had, the higher it ranked in search results and recommendations. This approach had several implications:

- **View Count:** Videos with high view counts quickly rose to prominence, often leading to viral content that attracted even more views.
- **Clickbait:** This era saw the rise of clickbait titles and thumbnails, as creators aimed to attract clicks without necessarily providing valuable or relevant content.
- **Engagement Metrics:** There was minimal focus on other engagement metrics like likes, comments, or watch time, which meant that videos were often not representative of quality or user satisfaction.

2. The Shift to Watch Time: 2012-2015

Recognizing the limitations of view counts, YouTube shifted its focus to watch time in 2012. This shift aimed to promote videos that kept viewers engaged longer, fostering the rise of longer-form and higher-quality content.

Watch time became a crucial metric as it measured the actual time users spent watching videos, indicating a deeper level of viewer interest and satisfaction than mere view counts could provide. This shift encouraged creators to prioritize content that captivated audiences and kept them on the platform, leading to more informative, entertaining, and engaging videos.

3. Introduction of Engagement Metrics: 2016-2017

By 2016, YouTube expanded its algorithm to incorporate a broader range of engagement metrics beyond watch time. Factors such as likes, dislikes, comments, and shares became significant indicators of viewer interaction and satisfaction.

.These metrics allowed YouTube to assess not only how long viewers watched videos but also how they responded to and interacted with the content. Videos that generated positive feedback, sparked discussions, and fostered community engagement were favored in search results and recommendations, promoting a more interactive and dynamic platform experience.

4. Focus on User Retention and Session Duration: 2018-Present

In recent years, YouTube has placed increased emphasis on user retention and session duration as key algorithmic metrics. User retention measures the percentage of viewers who continue watching a video after clicking on it, while session duration refers to the total time users spend on YouTube per session.

These metrics help determine how well a video or series of videos keep viewers engaged and contribute to prolonged user sessions on the platform.

YouTube's algorithm now prioritizes content that not only attracts initial clicks but also encourages prolonged viewing sessions, thereby enhancing overall user satisfaction and platform stickiness.

5. AI and Machine Learning Advancements

Throughout its evolution, YouTube has leveraged advancements in artificial intelligence (AI) and machine learning to refine its algorithm further. AI algorithms analyze vast amounts of data, including viewer behavior, content preferences, and trends, to deliver personalized recommendations in real-time. These algorithms continuously learn and adapt based on user interactions, improving the accuracy and relevance of content suggestions. AI-driven recommendations help YouTube users discover new content aligned with their interests, preferences, and viewing habits, thereby enhancing user engagement and satisfaction.

6. Impact on Content Creators and Viewers

The evolution of the YouTube algorithm has had profound implications for content creators and viewers alike. For creators, understanding and adapting to algorithmic changes are essential for effectively reaching and engaging their target audiences.

Strategies such as creating longer videos to increase watch time, encouraging viewer interactions through comments and likes, and optimizing content for user retention have become integral to success on the platform. Meanwhile, viewers benefit from a more personalized and engaging viewing experience, with access to content that aligns closely with their interests and preferences.

In conclusion, the history and evolution of the YouTube algorithm underscore YouTube's commitment to enhancing content discovery, viewer engagement, and overall platform experience. By continuously refining its algorithmic processes and leveraging AI technologies, YouTube strives to maintain its position as a leading platform for video content, fostering a dynamic and interactive community of creators and viewers worldwide.

This evolution reflects YouTube's dedication to providing relevant and high-quality content to its users, ensuring that creators who produce engaging and valuable content are rewarded with visibility and growth opportunities. As the platform continues to innovate, both creators and viewers benefit from a more personalized and satisfying user experience, solidifying YouTube's role as a premier destination for diverse and compelling video content.

Key Factors That Influence the Algorithm

The YouTube algorithm is a complex system designed to deliver personalized content to viewers, ensuring they find videos that are engaging and relevant to their interests. Understanding the key factors that influence the algorithm can help content creators optimize their videos for better visibility and engagement. Here are the main factors that play a crucial role:

1. Watch Time and Session Duration

Watch time is one of the most critical metrics influencing the YouTube algorithm. It measures the total amount of time viewers spend watching a video, indicating how engaging and valuable the content is. The algorithm favors videos that keep viewers engaged for longer periods, as this suggests high-quality content that meets viewer interests.

Additionally, session duration, which refers to the total time a user spends on YouTube during a single visit, is equally important. The algorithm rewards content that contributes to longer sessions, encouraging viewers to continue watching more videos on the platform. By focusing on creating compelling content that retains viewers and encourages extended viewing sessions, creators can significantly improve their video rankings and visibility.

2. Engagement Metrics

Engagement metrics, including likes, dislikes, comments, shares, and subscriptions, are vital indicators of how viewers interact with a video. These metrics reflect the audience's reaction and engagement level with the content.

Videos that receive high engagement are often favored by the algorithm, as they demonstrate active viewer interest and participation. Comments and shares, in particular, indicate deeper interaction and community involvement, signaling to the algorithm that the content is sparking meaningful conversations and connections.

Creators should encourage viewers to engage with their videos by asking questions, prompting discussions, and creating content that resonates emotionally or intellectually with their audience. Higher engagement not only boosts video rankings but also helps build a loyal and active viewer community.

3. Click-Through Rate (CTR) and Thumbnails

Click-through rate (CTR) is a crucial factor in determining a video's success on YouTube. CTR measures the percentage of viewers who click on a video after seeing its thumbnail and title.

indicates that the thumbnail and title are compelling and effectively capture viewers' attention. The algorithm uses CTR as a primary metric to assess the initial attractiveness of a video.

To optimize CTR, creators should design eye-catching and relevant thumbnails that accurately represent the video content while using intriguing and clear titles that entice viewers to click. Misleading thumbnails or titles, however, can lead to high initial clicks but poor watch time and engagement, which can negatively impact video rankings. Therefore, balancing attractiveness with accuracy is essential for maintaining both high CTR and viewer satisfaction.

In conclusion, watch time and session duration, engagement metrics, and click-through rate are key factors that significantly influence the YouTube algorithm. By focusing on these elements, content creators can enhance their video's visibility and engagement, leading to greater success on the platform.

Understanding and leveraging these factors helps creators align their content strategy with algorithmic preferences, ultimately building a stronger connection with their audience and fostering sustained growth on YouTube.

How the Algorithm Impacts Viewership

The YouTube algorithm plays a pivotal role in determining which videos get seen and how often they appear to viewers. Its influence on viewership is profound, as it directly affects content discovery, viewer engagement, and overall channel growth.

Understanding how the algorithm impacts viewership can help content creators strategically optimize their videos to reach a broader audience and enhance their presence on the platform. Here's a detailed exploration of the algorithm's impact on viewership:

1. Content Discovery and Recommendations

One of the primary ways the YouTube algorithm impacts viewership is through content discovery and recommendations. The algorithm is designed to predict and suggest videos that align with viewers' interests, behaviors, and past interactions on the platform. This includes personalized recommendations on the YouTube homepage, in the "Up Next" section, and within search results.

By analyzing factors such as watch history, search queries, and engagement patterns, the algorithm curates a selection of videos tailored to individual users.

This personalized approach increases the likelihood that viewers will discover and watch content that they find appealing, thereby boosting viewership for creators whose videos are recommended.

2. Influence of Trending and Popular Videos

The YouTube algorithm also highlights trending and popular videos, significantly impacting their viewership. Trending videos are those that rapidly gain a high number of views and engagement within a short period.

The algorithm features these videos on the Trending tab, making them more visible to a wider audience. Similarly, popular videos that consistently attract large viewership and high engagement rates are promoted more frequently across the platform.

This increased visibility can lead to exponential growth in views and subscribers for creators whose content resonates with a broad audience. However, achieving this level of exposure often requires creating content that is not only engaging but also timely and relevant to current trends.

3. Viewer Retention and Session Time

Viewer retention and session time are crucial metrics that the algorithm uses to evaluate the quality and relevance of a video.

High retention rates, where viewers watch a significant portion of a video, signal to the algorithm that the content is engaging and worth promoting. Similarly, videos that contribute to longer session times, where viewers continue watching other videos on the platform, are favored by the algorithm.

By prioritizing content that keeps viewers engaged and encourages extended viewing sessions, the algorithm helps maintain high user satisfaction and platform loyalty. Creators who focus on producing high-retention content can see substantial increases in viewership as their videos are promoted more frequently by the algorithm.

4. Impact of Audience Engagement

Audience engagement, measured through likes, dislikes, comments, shares, and subscriptions, significantly influences the algorithm's decisions.

High engagement levels indicate that viewers find the content interesting and valuable, prompting the algorithm to recommend it more often. Videos that spark conversations, generate feedback, and encourage social sharing can experience higher visibility and viewership.

Engaged audiences are more likely to interact with content regularly, contributing to sustained viewership growth.

Creators can boost engagement by actively responding to comments, encouraging discussions, and creating content that resonates emotionally or intellectually with their audience.

5. Algorithmic Changes and Adaptations

The YouTube algorithm is dynamic and continuously evolving, with periodic updates aimed at improving user experience and content discovery. These changes can significantly impact viewership patterns.

For example, shifts in algorithmic priorities, such as increased emphasis on watch time or user satisfaction, can alter which videos are promoted and how they are ranked. Creators need to stay informed about algorithmic updates and adapt their content strategies accordingly. By understanding the latest trends and adjustments in the algorithm, creators can optimize their videos to align with new priorities and maintain or enhance their viewership.

6. Impact on Niche and Diverse Content

The algorithm's focus on personalized recommendations also benefits niche and diverse content creators. By analyzing viewers' specific interests and preferences, the algorithm can surface niche content that might otherwise be overlooked.

This democratization of content discovery allows creators with unique or specialized topics to reach audiences who are genuinely interested in their content. As a result, even small or emerging channels can build a dedicated viewership and achieve significant growth through targeted algorithmic recommendations.

In conclusion, the YouTube algorithm has a profound impact on viewership by influencing content discovery, promoting trending and popular videos, enhancing viewer retention and session times, driving audience engagement, adapting to algorithmic changes, and supporting niche content.

By understanding these mechanisms, content creators can strategically optimize their videos to align with the algorithm's priorities, ultimately enhancing their visibility, engagement, and overall success on the platform.

This strategic alignment involves leveraging metadata, creating captivating thumbnails and titles, encouraging viewer interactions, and consistently producing high-quality content that meets audience expectations. By doing so, creators can navigate the complexities of the algorithm, maximize their reach, and build a loyal and engaged audience, ensuring their long-term success on YouTube.

Chapter 3
Creating Engaging Content

Types of Content That Perform Well

Creating content that resonates with viewers and aligns with YouTube's algorithmic priorities is essential for success on the platform. Certain types of content consistently perform well due to their ability to engage viewers, generate high watch time, and encourage interaction. Here's an in-depth look at various types of content that tend to thrive on YouTube:

1. Educational and How-To Videos
Educational and how-to videos are highly popular on YouTube as they provide valuable information and practical solutions to viewers. These videos range from tutorials on specific skills, such as cooking, DIY projects, and software usage, to in-depth explanations of complex topics.

The key to success in this category is delivering clear, concise, and actionable content that solves a problem or fulfills a need. Educational videos often achieve high watch times and engagement because viewers tend to watch them from start to finish to fully grasp the information being presented. Additionally, they are more likely to share and recommend useful tutorials to others, further boosting viewership.

2. Entertainment and Comedy

Entertainment and comedy videos are among the most viewed and shared content on YouTube. This category includes a wide range of formats, such as skits, parodies, stand-up routines, reaction videos, and challenges.

The primary goal is to entertain and amuse the audience, which often leads to high levels of engagement through likes, comments, and shares. Comedy and entertainment content have the potential to go viral, rapidly increasing viewership. Consistency in delivering humor and originality can help creators build a loyal fan base and achieve sustained success on the platform.

3. Vlogs and Personal Stories

Vlogs and personal stories offer a glimpse into the daily lives and experiences of creators, allowing viewers to connect on a more personal level. This type of content is characterized by its authenticity and relatability, as creators share their thoughts, adventures, challenges, and milestones.

Vlogs can cover a wide range of topics, from travel and lifestyle to personal growth and everyday routines. The intimate and candid nature of vlogs fosters a sense of community and belonging among viewers, leading to high engagement and long-term viewer loyalty. Creators who consistently share their unique perspectives and stories can build strong connections with their audience.

4. Product Reviews and Unboxings

Product reviews and unboxing videos are highly sought after by consumers looking for insights and opinions before making purchasing decisions. These videos provide detailed assessments of products, including their features, performance, and value for money.

Unboxing videos add an element of excitement and curiosity as creators unveil new products and share their first impressions. The trust and credibility established through honest and thorough reviews can lead to high viewer retention and engagement. Additionally, product review channels often attract sponsorships and partnerships with brands, providing additional revenue opportunities for creators.

5. Gaming Content

Gaming content is one of the most vibrant and active categories on YouTube. This includes gameplay walkthroughs, live streams, game reviews, and commentary. Gamers often build large and dedicated followings by showcasing their skills, sharing tips and strategies, and providing entertaining commentary.

The interactive nature of gaming content, particularly through live streams, fosters a strong sense of community among viewers. Gaming channels can achieve high watch times and engagement due to the immersive and engaging nature of the content.

6. Health and Fitness

Health and fitness videos cater to the growing interest in wellness and self-improvement. This category includes workout routines, nutrition advice, mental health tips, and holistic lifestyle practices.

Creators who offer expertise, motivation, and guidance can attract a dedicated audience seeking to improve their health and well-being. High-quality, effective, and varied fitness routines can lead to high watch times and repeat viewership. Engaging with viewers through challenges, progress updates, and community support can enhance interaction and build a loyal following.

7. Music and Performance

Music and performance videos encompass a wide range of content, including music videos, covers, live performances, and original compositions. This category attracts viewers who appreciate talent and creativity in music and performing arts.

Musicians and performers can achieve widespread recognition and viral success by showcasing their skills and creativity. Collaborations with other artists and participation in musical trends can enhance visibility and reach. High production quality, originality, and emotional connection are key factors in attracting and retaining viewers in this category.

8. News and Commentary

News and commentary channels provide analysis, opinions, and updates on current events, politics, and social issues. These channels attract viewers who seek informed perspectives and discussions on relevant topics.

Timely and well-researched content can lead to high viewer retention and engagement, as viewers rely on these channels for accurate and insightful information. Encouraging discussions through comments and live interactions can foster a sense of community and engagement among viewers.

9. Lifestyle and Travel

Lifestyle and travel videos offer viewers an escape and inspiration by showcasing different cultures, destinations, and ways of living. These videos often feature stunning visuals, personal experiences, and practical tips for travel and lifestyle improvements.

Creators who share their adventures, cultural insights, and lifestyle choices can attract a diverse and engaged audience. High production quality, storytelling, and authenticity are crucial for success in this category. Viewers are drawn to the aspirational and informative nature of lifestyle and travel content, leading to high engagement and repeat viewership.

10. Science and Technology

Science and technology videos appeal to viewers interested in innovation, discoveries, and advancements in various fields. This category includes tech reviews, scientific explanations, DIY tech projects, and exploration of futuristic concepts.

Creators who break down complex topics into understandable and engaging content can attract a dedicated audience of tech enthusiasts and curious minds. High-quality visuals, clear explanations, and staying updated with the latest trends and developments are essential for success in this category. The educational and informative nature of science and technology videos often leads to high watch times and engagement.

In conclusion, educational and how-to videos, entertainment and comedy, vlogs and personal stories, product reviews and unboxings, gaming content, health and fitness, music and performance, news and commentary, lifestyle and travel, and science and technology are types of content that consistently perform well on YouTube.

By understanding the preferences and behaviors of their target audience and aligning their content strategy with these successful formats, creators can enhance their visibility, engagement, and overall success on the platform.

Crafting Captivating Titles and Thumbnails

Titles and thumbnails are the first things potential viewers see when they come across a video on YouTube. They play a critical role in attracting attention, enticing clicks, and setting expectations for the content.

Crafting captivating titles and thumbnails can significantly enhance a video's click-through rate (CTR) and overall success on the platform. Here's a detailed exploration of how to create engaging titles and thumbnails:

1. Understanding the Importance

Titles and thumbnails serve as the primary gateway to your video. They need to stand out in a sea of content and compel viewers to click. A well-crafted title and thumbnail combination can:

- **Increase Click-Through Rates (CTR):** A higher CTR indicates that more people are choosing to watch your video after seeing it in search results or recommendations.
- **Set Viewer Expectations:** They give viewers a clear idea of what to expect, ensuring that the content matches their interests and needs.
- **Boost Video Rankings:** Higher CTR and viewer retention can improve your video's ranking in search results and recommendations, leading to more views.

2. Crafting Compelling Titles

A captivating title is concise, informative, and intriguing. Here are some key strategies for creating effective titles:

A. Keep It Clear and Concise

- **Be Specific:** Clearly describe what the video is about. For example, "How to Bake a Perfect Chocolate Cake" is more specific than "Baking Tips."
- **Use Keywords:** Incorporate relevant keywords that viewers are likely to search for. This improves your video's visibility in search results.

B. Create Curiosity and Interest

- **Pose a Question:** Titles that ask a question can spark curiosity. For instance, "Can You Survive on $10 a Day? Travel Challenge!"
- **Use Numbers and Lists:** Numbers can make titles more attractive. Examples include "10 Tips for Perfect Hair Every Day" or "Top 5 Budget Travel Destinations."

C. Highlight the Value

- **Promise a Benefit:** Show viewers what they will gain from watching the video. For example, "Boost Your Productivity: 5 Simple Habits" promises a clear benefit.

- **Use Power Words:** Words like "ultimate," "essential," "amazing," and "secret" can make titles more compelling. For example, "The Ultimate Guide to Weight Loss."

D. Keep It Authentic
Avoid Clickbait: Ensure your title accurately reflects the content. Misleading titles may attract clicks but can lead to poor viewer retention and negative feedback.

3. Designing Eye-Catching Thumbnails
Thumbnails are visual representations of your video and need to be both attractive and informative. Here are some best practices for creating effective thumbnails:

A. Use High-Quality Images
Clear and Bright: Ensure the image is clear, bright, and high-resolution. Blurry or dark images are less likely to attract clicks.
Relevant to the Content: The image should accurately represent the video's content to set proper expectations.

B. Include Text Overlays

- **Complement the Title:** Use short, punchy text that complements the title. For example, a video titled "Easy Home Workouts" could have a thumbnail with the text "No Equipment Needed!"

- **Readable Fonts:** Use bold, easy-to-read fonts and contrasting colors to ensure the text stands out.

C. Leverage Faces and Emotions

- **Human Faces:** Thumbnails featuring faces, especially with expressive emotions, can attract more clicks. People are naturally drawn to faces and emotions.
- **Engaging Expressions:** Use expressions that match the video's tone, whether it's excitement, surprise, or seriousness.

D. Maintain Consistent Branding

- **Brand Elements:** Incorporate elements like your logo, brand colors, or consistent style to make your thumbnails recognizable.
- **Uniform Style:** A consistent style helps build a visual identity and makes your videos easily identifiable in search results and recommendations.

E. Test and Optimize

- **A/B Testing:** Experiment with different thumbnail designs and titles to see which ones perform better. YouTube's analytics can help you understand what works best.
- **Analyze Performance:** Regularly review performance metrics such as CTR and average watch time to refine your strategy.

4. Combining Titles and Thumbnails

The combination of titles and thumbnails should work together to attract and inform potential viewers. Here are some tips for ensuring they complement each other:

A. Consistent Messaging

- **Aligned Content:** Ensure the title and thumbnail convey the same message and accurately represent the video content.
- **Unified Theme:** Use similar colors, fonts, and styles to create a cohesive look that enhances brand recognition.

B. Highlighting Key Points

- **Reinforce Key Points:** Use the thumbnail to highlight key aspects of the title. For instance, if the title is "5-Minute Makeup Hacks," the thumbnail could feature a close-up of makeup products or the finished look.

C. Previewing the Content

- **Tease the Content:** Give viewers a glimpse of what to expect without revealing everything. This can intrigue them enough to click and watch the video.

crafting captivating titles and thumbnails is crucial for attracting viewers and enhancing video performance on YouTube.

By understanding their importance, creating clear and engaging titles, designing eye-catching thumbnails, and ensuring they work together seamlessly, content creators can significantly improve their video's visibility, engagement, and overall success on the platform.

Titles and thumbnails are often the first impression a potential viewer has of your content, making them critical elements in attracting clicks. A compelling title should be concise yet descriptive, incorporating relevant keywords that improve searchability. Thumbnails, on the other hand, should be visually appealing, accurately representing the video's content, and featuring bold text or imagery that stands out. When these two elements are harmoniously integrated, they create a cohesive and enticing preview that encourages viewers to click and watch.

Furthermore, effective titles and thumbnails contribute to higher click-through rates (CTR), which is a key metric in YouTube's algorithm for recommending videos. A high CTR signals to the algorithm that your content is engaging and relevant, increasing the likelihood of it being suggested to more viewers.

Importance of High-Quality Production

High-quality production is a key element in creating successful YouTube content. As the platform becomes increasingly competitive, viewers have come to expect professional, polished videos that provide an enjoyable viewing experience. Investing in high-quality production can significantly impact viewer retention, engagement, and overall channel growth. Here's a detailed exploration of the importance of high-quality production:

1. First Impressions Matter

The first few seconds of a video are crucial in capturing and retaining viewer attention. High-quality production ensures that your video makes a strong first impression. Here's how it matters:

A. Visual Appeal

- **Clear and Sharp Images:** High-resolution video with clear, sharp images is more visually appealing and engaging. Viewers are more likely to continue watching if the video looks professional and aesthetically pleasing.
- **Good Lighting:** Proper lighting enhances the visual quality, making the video more attractive and easier to watch. It helps highlight important details and creates a professional look.

B. Audio Quality

- **Clear Audio:** Clear, crisp audio is essential for viewer comprehension and engagement. Poor audio quality can be distracting and may cause viewers to abandon the video.
- **Balanced Sound Levels:** Proper sound mixing ensures that dialogue, music, and sound effects are balanced, preventing any one element from overpowering the others.

C. Professional Presentation

- **Smooth Transitions:** Professional transitions and editing techniques contribute to a polished look, making the video more enjoyable to watch.
- **Consistent Branding:** Consistent use of branding elements, such as logos and color schemes, reinforces brand identity and makes your content more recognizable.

2. Enhancing Viewer Engagement

High-quality production plays a significant role in enhancing viewer engagement, which is critical for retaining audience attention and encouraging interaction. Here's how it impacts engagement:

A. Visual and Audio Clarity

- **Improved Comprehension:** High-quality visuals and audio make it easier for viewers to understand and follow the content. This leads to higher retention rates and encourages viewers to watch longer.
- **Reduced Distractions:** Professional production minimizes distractions caused by poor lighting, shaky camera work, or background noise, allowing viewers to focus on the content.

B. Emotional Connection

- **Storytelling:** High-quality production supports effective storytelling by using visuals, music, and sound effects to evoke emotions and create a compelling narrative. This emotional connection can lead to higher engagement and viewer loyalty.
- **Relatability:** Professional production helps convey your message more effectively, making it easier for viewers to relate to the content and feel connected to the creator. High-quality visuals and clear audio enhance the viewing experience, allowing the audience to focus on the message without distractions. Well-edited videos that flow smoothly and incorporate engaging elements, such as graphics or relevant cutaways, can also hold viewers' attention better.

C. Viewer Interaction

- **Encouraging Feedback:** Well-produced videos are more likely to receive positive feedback, likes, and comments, which are important engagement metrics.
- **Sharing and Recommendations:** High-quality content is more likely to be shared and recommended by viewers, expanding your reach and attracting new audiences.

3. Building Credibility and Trust

High-quality production helps establish credibility and trust with your audience, which is essential for building a loyal viewer base. Here's why it matters:

A. Professionalism

- **Credible Image:** Professional-looking videos convey a sense of credibility and expertise. Viewers are more likely to trust and value content that appears well-produced and polished.
- **Brand Authority:** Consistently high-quality production reinforces your brand's authority and reputation, making viewers more likely to return for future content.

B. Viewer Trust

- **Reliability:** High-quality production signals to viewers that you are serious about your content and committed to providing a reliable, enjoyable experience.
- **Consistency:** Maintaining consistent production quality helps build viewer trust, as they know what to expect from your videos in terms of visual and audio standards.

4. Enhancing Content Discoverability

High-quality production can also impact your content's discoverability on YouTube, contributing to greater visibility and growth. Here's how:

A. Algorithm Favorability

- **Retention and Watch Time:** High-quality videos are more likely to retain viewers for longer periods, boosting metrics like watch time and viewer retention. These metrics are important factors in YouTube's algorithm for recommending content.
- **Engagement Metrics:** Videos with high production value tend to receive more likes, comments, and shares, further signaling to the algorithm that your content is valuable and worth promoting.

B. SEO and Thumbnails

- **Appealing Thumbnails:** High-quality production allows for the creation of visually appealing thumbnails, which can improve click-through rates (CTR) and attract more viewers.
- **SEO Optimization:** Well-produced videos often include clear, concise titles, descriptions, and tags, enhancing their searchability and discoverability on the platform.

5. Long-Term Channel Growth

Investing in high-quality production contributes to the long-term growth and success of your YouTube channel. Here's how it supports growth:

A. Audience Retention

- **Loyal Viewership:** High-quality content encourages viewers to subscribe and return for future videos, fostering a loyal audience base.
- **Increased Watch Time:** Consistently high production standards lead to higher watch times, which are crucial for channel growth and monetization. When videos are well-produced, with clear audio, sharp visuals, and engaging editing, viewers are more likely to stay engaged and watch the content for longer periods.

B. Monetization Opportunities

- **Ad Revenue:** Higher viewer retention and engagement can lead to increased ad revenue, as advertisers prefer to place ads on well-produced, high-engagement videos.
- **Brand Partnerships:** High-quality production attracts sponsorships and partnerships with brands looking to collaborate with credible and professional creators.

In conclusion, high-quality production is essential for making a strong first impression, enhancing viewer engagement, building credibility and trust, improving content discoverability, and supporting long-term channel growth.

By investing in professional visuals, audio, and editing, content creators can significantly enhance their videos' appeal and effectiveness, leading to greater success on YouTube. High-quality visuals make content more visually appealing and can help convey messages more clearly, while crisp and clear audio ensures that viewers can easily understand and engage with the content. Effective editing can keep the audience's attention by maintaining a smooth and engaging flow, cutting out unnecessary parts, and adding elements like graphics, music, and transitions to enhance the overall viewing experience.

Chapter 4
Keywords and SEO for YouTube

Conducting Keyword Research

Keyword research is a fundamental aspect of optimizing YouTube videos for search and discovery. By identifying and using the right keywords, content creators can improve their video's visibility, attract more viewers, and grow their channel. Here's an in-depth look at the process and importance of conducting keyword research:

1. Understanding the Importance of Keyword Research

Keyword research helps you understand what terms and phrases your potential viewers are searching for on YouTube. Here's why it's essential:

A. Enhancing Visibility

- **Search Rankings:** Using relevant keywords in your video title, description, and tags can improve your video's ranking in YouTube search results, making it easier for viewers to find your content.

- **Suggested Videos:** Optimized keywords help your video appear in the suggested video section, increasing the chances of being discovered by viewers watching similar content.

B. Targeting the Right Audience

- **Relevance:** By identifying keywords that your target audience is searching for, you can create content that directly addresses their interests and needs, increasing viewer engagement and satisfaction.
- **Intent:** Understanding the search intent behind keywords allows you to tailor your content to meet viewers' expectations, whether they are looking for information, entertainment, or solutions.

C. Competitive Advantage

- **Niche Opportunities:** Keyword research can help you identify underserved topics within your niche, allowing you to create content that fills gaps in the market and attracts a dedicated audience.
- **Trend Identification:** Keeping up with trending keywords can help you stay relevant and produce timely content that captures current viewer interest.

2. Steps to Conduct Effective Keyword Research

Conducting effective keyword research involves several steps, each aimed at discovering the best keywords to use for your content. Here's a detailed guide to the process:

A. Brainstorming Initial Ideas

- **Topic Relevance:** Start by brainstorming topics relevant to your channel and audience. Consider what your viewers are interested in and what problems they want to solve.
- **Viewer Questions:** Think about common questions or issues your viewers might have that you can address in your videos.

B. Using Keyword Research Tools

- **YouTube Search Bar:** Use the YouTube search bar to see auto-suggested keywords as you type. These suggestions are based on popular searches and can provide insights into what viewers are looking for.
- **Google Trends:** Analyze the popularity of search terms over time to identify trending topics and seasonal interests.
- **Keyword Planner Tools:** Tools like Google Keyword Planner, Ahrefs, and TubeBuddy offer comprehensive keyword research features, including search volume, competition level, and related keywords.

C. Analyzing Competitor Content

- **Top Performing Videos:** Look at the top-performing videos in your niche to see what keywords they are using in their titles, descriptions, and tags.
- **Common Keywords:** Identify common keywords and phrases used by successful creators to understand what works well in your niche.

D. Refining Keyword Choices

- **Relevance and Specificity:** Choose keywords that are highly relevant to your content and specific enough to attract targeted viewers. Long-tail keywords (phrases with three or more words) are often more effective because they have less competition and a clearer search intent.
- **Search Volume and Competition:** Balance between keywords with high search volume and those with manageable competition. High-volume keywords can bring more traffic, but low-competition keywords might offer better chances of ranking higher.

3. Incorporating Keywords into Your Content

Once you've identified the right keywords, it's crucial to incorporate them strategically into your content to optimize for search and discovery:

A. Titles

- **Primary Keyword Placement:** Place the primary keyword at the beginning of your video title for maximum impact. For example, "How to Bake a Perfect Chocolate Cake - Easy Recipe" emphasizes "How to Bake a Perfect Chocolate Cake" as the primary keyword.
- **Compelling and Descriptive:** Ensure your title is not only keyword-rich but also compelling and descriptive to attract clicks.

B. Descriptions

- **First 200 Characters:** The first 200 characters of your video description are critical for SEO. Include your primary keyword here and provide a brief overview of the video content.
- **Detailed Description:** Write a detailed description that includes secondary keywords and related phrases naturally. Explain what the video is about, what viewers will learn, and why it's valuable.

C. Tags

- **Relevant Tags:** Use relevant tags that reflect the content of your video. Include both primary and secondary keywords as well as related terms.
- **Mix of Specific and Broad Tags:** Use a mix of specific (long-tail) and broad (short-tail) tags to cover various search queries.

D. Transcripts and Closed Captions

- **Transcripts:** Uploading accurate transcripts can help YouTube understand the content of your video better and improve its SEO.
- **Closed Captions:** Adding closed captions enhances accessibility and can also boost your video's SEO by making it easier for YouTube to index your content.

E. Thumbnails and Metadata

- **Text in Thumbnails:** Including keywords or key phrases in your thumbnail text can reinforce the video's relevance and attract more clicks.
- **Metadata Optimization:** Ensure all metadata (titles, descriptions, tags) is fully optimized with the keywords you've researched.

4. Monitoring and Adjusting Your Strategy

Keyword research is an ongoing process. Regularly monitoring your video performance and adjusting your strategy based on the insights you gain is crucial:

A. Analyzing Performance

- **YouTube Analytics:** Use YouTube Analytics to track the performance of your videos. Pay attention to metrics like views, watch time, and CTR to see how well your keywords are performing.

Traffic Sources: Analyze traffic sources to understand where your viewers are coming from and which keywords are driving the most traffic.

B. Adapting to Trends

- **Trend Monitoring:** Stay updated with current trends and adjust your content strategy to incorporate trending keywords when relevant.
- **Content Updates:** Periodically update older videos with new keywords and improved descriptions to keep them relevant and boost their visibility.

C. Continuous Improvement

- **Experimentation:** Continuously experiment with different keywords and content formats to see what works best for your audience.
- **Feedback Loop:** Use viewer feedback and engagement metrics to refine your keyword strategy and content approach.

conducting keyword research is vital for optimizing your YouTube videos for search and discovery. By understanding the importance of keywords, following a systematic research process, strategically incorporating keywords into your content, and regularly monitoring and adjusting your strategy, you can significantly enhance your video's visibility, attract more viewers, and achieve long-term success on YouTube.

Optimizing Video Titles and Descriptions

Optimizing video titles and descriptions is crucial for improving the visibility of your YouTube content, attracting more viewers, and enhancing engagement. Well-crafted titles and descriptions not only help your videos rank higher in search results but also provide viewers with clear and compelling reasons to watch your content. Here's an in-depth look at how to effectively optimize your video titles and descriptions:

1. Crafting Effective Titles

A compelling title is the first thing potential viewers see and plays a vital role in whether they click on your video. Here's how to craft effective titles:

A. Incorporate Primary Keywords

- **Keyword Placement:** Place your primary keyword at the beginning of the title for maximum impact. This helps with SEO and makes it clear what your video is about.
- **Relevance:** Ensure the keywords are highly relevant to the content of your video to attract the right audience. Keywords play a crucial role in helping YouTube understand the context and subject matter of your video, which in turn influences where and to whom it gets recommended.

B. Keep It Concise and Clear

- **Short and Sweet:** Aim for titles that are concise yet descriptive. YouTube typically displays the first 60 characters of a title, so make sure the essential information fits within this limit.
- **Avoid Overly Long Titles:** Long titles can be truncated in search results, which might cut off important information.

C. Create Curiosity and Interest

- **Engaging Phrases:** Use engaging phrases and power words to spark curiosity. Words like "how to," "tips," "secrets," "ultimate," and "guide" can attract viewers.
- **Questions:** Posing a question in the title can intrigue viewers and prompt them to click. For example, "Can You Solve This Riddle?"

D. Highlight the Value Proposition

- **Benefits and Value:** Clearly convey the benefit or value of watching the video. For instance, "Learn How to Bake a Perfect Cake in 10 Minutes" emphasizes the value of quick and easy baking tips.
- **Unique Selling Points:** Highlight what makes your video unique compared to others on the same topic.

E. Maintain Authenticity

- **Avoid Clickbait:** Ensure your title accurately represents the content of the video. Misleading titles may attract clicks initially but can lead to negative viewer feedback and lower retention rates.
- **Genuine Content:** Authentic and honest titles build trust with your audience, encouraging them to return for more content.

2. Writing Detailed Descriptions

Video descriptions provide additional context about your content and are essential for SEO. Here's how to write detailed and effective descriptions:

A. Start with a Strong Introduction

- **Primary Keyword:** Include your primary keyword within the first 200 characters of the description. This section is crucial for SEO as it appears in search results.
- **Brief Summary:** Provide a brief summary of the video content to capture the viewer's interest right away. A concise and compelling summary in the first few sentences of your video description can encourage viewers to click and watch. Clearly outline what the video is about, what viewers will learn or experience, and why it's valuable to them.

B. Provide Comprehensive Details

- **Extended Description:** Write a more detailed description that expands on what the video covers. Include key points, important topics, and any additional context that might be relevant.
- **Secondary Keywords:** Naturally incorporate secondary keywords and related phrases throughout the description to improve searchability.

C. Include Links and Resources

- **External Links:** Provide links to your website, social media profiles, and related content. This can drive traffic to your other platforms and offer viewers more ways to engage with your content.
- **Internal Links:** Link to other videos or playlists on your channel that are relevant to the current video. This can help increase watch time and keep viewers on your channel longer.

D. Use Timestamps for Longer Videos

- **Timestamps:** For longer videos, include timestamps in the description to help viewers navigate to specific sections of the video. This improves user experience and retention.
- **Chapter Titles:** Name each timestamped section descriptively to give viewers an idea of what to expect.

E. Encourage Viewer Engagement

- **Calls to Action:** Encourage viewers to like, comment, and subscribe within your description. Phrases like "Let us know your thoughts in the comments" or "Subscribe for more content" can prompt engagement.
- **Questions:** Pose a question related to the video content to encourage comments and discussions.

F. Utilize YouTube's Additional Features

- **Hashtags:** Use relevant hashtags at the end of your description. YouTube allows up to 15 hashtags, and they can help improve discoverability.
- **Default Upload Settings:** Set default descriptions for all your uploads to ensure consistency. You can always customize each one as needed. By creating a standardized template for video descriptions, you streamline your workflow and maintain a professional appearance across your channel. Include key information such as links to your social media profiles, relevant playlists, and a call to action (CTA) encouraging viewers to subscribe or engage with your content further. This approach not only saves time but also ensures that important details are consistently communicated to your audience.

3. Best Practices for Optimization

Following these best practices will help you optimize your titles and descriptions effectively:

A. Consistency and Branding

- **Consistent Style:** Maintain a consistent style and tone in your titles and descriptions to build a recognizable brand identity.
- **Branding Elements:** Incorporate branding elements such as your channel name or slogan to reinforce brand recognition.

B. Testing and Refining

- **A/B Testing:** Experiment with different titles and descriptions to see what resonates best with your audience. YouTube Analytics can provide insights into what's working.
- **Performance Monitoring:** Regularly review the performance of your videos and make adjustments based on viewer engagement and retention metrics.

C. Keeping Up with Trends

- **Trend Awareness:** Stay updated with current trends and incorporate trending keywords and topics into your titles and descriptions when relevant.

- **Timely Updates:** Update older video descriptions with new keywords and information to keep them relevant and improve their performance.

D. Utilizing Tools and Resources

- **Keyword Tools:** Use tools like Google Keyword Planner, TubeBuddy, and vidIQ to research and identify the best keywords for your content.
- **SEO Plugins:** Leverage SEO plugins and extensions to analyze and optimize your titles and descriptions more effectively.

4. Examples of Optimized Titles and Descriptions

Here are some examples to illustrate effective optimization:

A. Title Examples

- How to Bake a Perfect Chocolate Cake – Easy Step-by-Step Guide
- Top 10 Travel Destinations for 2024 – Ultimate Travel Guide
- Quick Home Workouts for Beginners – No Equipment Needed!
- Healthy Breakfast Recipes Under 10 Minutes – Easy and Nutritious Ideas
- Photography Tips for Beginners – Capturing Stunning Photos with Your Smartphone
- Financial Planning 101 – Budgeting, Saving, and Investing for Long-Term Success

B. Description Examples

How to Bake a Perfect Chocolate Cake Easy Stepby Step Guide:

In this video, we'll show you how to bake the perfect chocolate cake from scratch. Follow our easy, step-by-step guide to create a delicious and moist cake that everyone will love. Starting with the finest ingredients and essential techniques, we'll guide you through each stage of the baking process, ensuring your cake turns out beautifully every time. Whether you're a baking novice or seasoned enthusiast, this tutorial is designed to simplify the baking experience and guarantee impressive results.

Don't forget to like this video if you find it helpful, comment below with your baking experiences, and subscribe to our channel for more delightful baking tips and recipes!

Check out our website for the full recipe: [link]
Follow us on Instagram: [link]
Watch our other baking videos: [link]

#Baking #ChocolateCake #Recipe"

Top 10 Travel Destinations for 2024 – Ultimate Travel Guide:

"Planning your next vacation? Here are the top 10 travel destinations for 2024 that you must visit. From tropical beaches to vibrant cities, we've got you covered with all the best places to explore. Let us know your favorite travel destination in the comments!

Visit our travel blog for more tips: [link]
Join our travel community on Facebook: [link]
Watch more travel guides: [link]

0:00 Introduction
0:45 Destination #1: Bali, Indonesia
3:20 Destination #2: Kyoto, Japan
6:05 Destination #3: Santorini, Greece

In conclusion, optimizing video titles and descriptions is essential for improving search visibility, attracting viewers, and enhancing engagement on YouTube. By crafting clear, concise, and compelling titles, writing detailed and informative descriptions, and following best practices, you can significantly boost the performance of your videos and grow your channel.

Utilizing Tags Effectively

Utilizing tags effectively is a crucial part of optimizing your YouTube videos for searchability and discoverability. Tags help YouTube understand the content of your video, ensuring it appears in relevant search results and suggested videos. Here's an in-depth guide on how to use tags effectively:

1. Understanding the Role of Tags

Tags are descriptive keywords or phrases that provide context about your video to YouTube's algorithm. Here's why they are important:

A. Enhancing Search Visibility

- **SEO Optimization:** Tags help improve your video's SEO by signaling to YouTube what your video is about. This can boost your ranking in search results.
- **Relevance Matching:** Properly tagged videos are more likely to appear in related video suggestions, increasing the chances of being discovered by viewers interested in similar content. Tags play a crucial role in YouTube's algorithm, helping to categorize and connect your video with relevant topics and themes. When selecting tags, consider keywords that accurately describe the content of your video and align with what your target audience is searching for.

B. Improving Content Categorization

- **Algorithm Understanding:** Tags assist YouTube's algorithm in categorizing your video correctly, ensuring it reaches the right audience.
- **Context Clarity:** They provide additional context that might not be fully captured by the title and description alone.

2. Choosing the Right Tags

Choosing the right tags involves research and strategic thinking to ensure they accurately reflect your content and attract the right audience. Here's how to select effective tags:

A. Primary Keywords

- **Primary Focus**: Use your primary keyword as the first tag. This should be the main topic or theme of your video.
- **Exact Matches:** Include exact match keywords that users are likely to search for. These keywords should directly reflect the specific topics, phrases, or questions that your video addresses. By incorporating exact match keywords in your video title, description, and tags, you increase the likelihood of your content appearing prominently in search results when viewers enter those exact queries.

B. Secondary Keywords

- **Related Phrases**: Use secondary keywords that are related to your primary keyword. These should cover variations and related terms viewers might use.
- **Synonyms:** Incorporate synonyms and alternative phrases to capture a broader range of search queries.

C. Long-Tail Keywords

- **Specific Phrases:** Long-tail keywords are more specific and usually consist of three or more words. These can help target a niche audience and often have less competition.
- **Detailed Tags:** Use detailed tags that describe specific aspects of your content. For example, "how to bake a chocolate cake from scratch" instead of just "cake."

D. Broad Tags

- **General Terms:** Include a few broad tags that cover general categories related to your video. These can help place your video in a wider context.
- **Trending Topics:** Incorporate trending keywords if they are relevant to your content to capture timely search traffic.

E. Competitor Analysis

- **Analyze Top Videos:** Look at the tags used by top-performing videos in your niche. This can provide insights into what works and help you discover additional relevant tags.
- **Common Themes:** Identify common themes and keywords among successful videos and consider incorporating them into your tags.

3. Strategic Tag Implementation

Implementing your tags strategically involves organizing and prioritizing them effectively. Here's how to do it:

A. Prioritize Relevance

- **Order of Importance:** Place the most important and relevant tags at the beginning of your list. YouTube's algorithm places more weight on the first few tags.
- **Focus on Core Content:** Ensure the first tags directly relate to the core content of your video. These initial tags should accurately represent the main topic, theme, or focus of your video. By prioritizing tags that align closely with the primary subject matter, you optimize your video's relevance and visibility within YouTube's search and recommendation systems. This strategic tagging not only helps attract viewers who are specifically interested in your content but also enhances the likelihood of your video being recommended alongside similar videos.

B. Use a Mix of Tags

- **Balanced Approach:** Use a balanced mix of primary, secondary, long-tail, and broad tags to cover various aspects of your video.
- **Avoid Overloading:** While it's tempting to use as many tags as possible, avoid overloading your video with irrelevant tags. This can confuse the algorithm and dilute your video's relevance.

C. Consistent Tagging

- **Channel Consistency:** Maintain consistent tagging across your videos to help YouTube understand your content niche and improve overall channel discoverability.
- **Revisit and Update:** Periodically revisit and update your tags based on new insights, trends, and video performance analytics.

4. Best Practices for Tagging

Following best practices can help you maximize the effectiveness of your tags:

A. Be Descriptive and Specific

- **Clear Descriptions:** Use tags that clearly describe the content of your video. Specific tags help YouTube categorize your video more accurately.

- **Avoid Generic Terms:** Generic terms like "fun" or "interesting" are too broad and don't provide valuable information about your content.

B. Use YouTube's Suggested Tags

- **Auto-Suggestions:** Utilize YouTube's auto-suggest feature to find popular and relevant tags. These suggestions are based on what users are currently searching for.
- **Trending Tags:** Incorporate trending tags when appropriate to capture current search interest.

C. Keep Audience in Mind

- **Viewer Intent:** Consider what your target audience would search for when looking for content like yours. Align your tags with viewer search intent.
- **User Language:** Use language and terminology that your audience uses. This ensures your tags resonate with their search behavior.

D. Avoid Tag Stuffing

- **Quality Over Quantity:** Focus on the quality of your tags rather than quantity. Using too many tags, especially irrelevant ones, can confuse the algorithm and reduce your video's effectiveness.
- **Relevance:** Ensure all tags are relevant to your video content to maintain clarity and focus.

E. Use Tools and Resources

- **Keyword Tools:** Utilize tools like TubeBuddy, VidIQ, and Google Keyword Planner to find effective tags and analyze their performance.
- **Analytics:** Regularly check your YouTube Analytics to see which tags are driving traffic and adjust your strategy accordingly.

5. Examples of Effective Tagging

Here are examples of effective tagging for different types of content:

A. Cooking Tutorial: "How to Bake a Perfect Chocolate Cake"

- **Primary Tag:** "chocolate cake recipe"
- **Secondary Tags:** "how to bake a cake," "baking tips," "easy cake recipes," "homemade chocolate cake"
- **Long-Tail Tags:** "how to bake a chocolate cake from scratch," "best chocolate cake recipe for beginners"
- **Broad Tags:** "baking," "desserts," "cooking tutorials"

B. Travel Vlog: "Top 10 Travel Destinations for 2024"

- **Primary Tag:** "top travel destinations 2024"
- **Secondary Tags:** "best places to visit," "travel guide," "holiday destinations," "travel tips"

- **Long-Tail Tags:** "top 10 travel destinations 2024," "where to travel in 2024," "best holiday destinations 2024"
- **Broad Tags:** "travel," "vacation," "tourism"

C. Fitness Video: "Quick Home Workouts for Beginners"

- **Primary Tag:** "home workouts"
- **Secondary Tags:** "beginner workouts," "quick workouts," "exercise at home," "no equipment workouts"
- **Long-Tail Tags:** "quick home workouts for beginners," "easy workouts for beginners at home," "10-minute home workouts"
- **Broad Tags:** "fitness," "exercise," "health"

In conclusion, utilizing tags effectively is vital for enhancing your video's discoverability and reaching the right audience on YouTube. By understanding the role of tags, choosing the right keywords, implementing them strategically, following best practices, and learning from examples, you can optimize your videos for better search results and increased viewer engagement.Following best practices such as using a mix of broad and specific tags, incorporating trending or seasonal keywords when relevant, and updating tags periodically to reflect changing viewer interests can further enhance your video's visibility over time.

Chapter 5
The Role of Watch Time

What is Watch Time and Why It Matters

Watch time is one of the most crucial metrics on YouTube. It measures the total amount of time viewers spend watching your videos. Unlike views, which simply count the number of times a video is played, watch time provides a more comprehensive understanding of how engaging and valuable your content is to your audience. Here's an in-depth look at what watch time is and why it matters:

1. Defining Watch Time
Watch time refers to the cumulative minutes or hours that viewers spend watching your videos. It is a key performance indicator (KPI) that YouTube uses to evaluate the success and popularity of a video or channel. Watch time is calculated by summing the duration of all individual viewing sessions of a video. This metric is significant because it reflects how engaging and valuable your content is to viewers. Videos with higher watch times signal to YouTube's algorithm that they are worth promoting, as they keep viewers on the platform longer and contribute to a positive user experience.

A. Total Watch Time

Channel Level: This is the total amount of watch time accumulated across all videos on your channel over a specific period.
Video Level: This refers to the total watch time of a specific video.

B. Average Watch Time

- **Per View:** The average amount of time a viewer spends watching a video in a single viewing session.
- **Retention Metrics:** This includes metrics like average view duration and audience retention, which provide insights into how well your video retains viewers' attention.

2. Why Watch Time Matters

Watch time is a critical metric for several reasons, all of which impact your channel's performance, growth, and revenue potential.

A. Algorithm Preference

- **YouTube's Algorithm:** YouTube's algorithm prioritizes videos with higher watch time. Videos that keep viewers engaged for longer periods are more likely to be promoted through search results, suggested videos, and the homepage.

User Experience: High watch time signals to YouTube that viewers find your content valuable and engaging, which enhances the user experience.

B. Monetization Potential

- **Ad Revenue:** Longer watch times can lead to higher ad revenue. Videos that retain viewers for extended periods allow more ads to be served, increasing your earning potential.
- **Channel Memberships:** Channels with consistently high watch times are more likely to attract subscribers and members, contributing to a steady income stream.

C. Viewer Engagement and Loyalty

- **Engaged Audience:** Videos with higher watch times typically indicate a more engaged audience. Engaged viewers are more likely to like, comment, share, and subscribe to your channel.
- **Community Building:** Sustained viewer engagement helps in building a loyal community around your content, leading to long-term channel growth. When viewers regularly watch, like, comment, and share your videos, they become more invested in your channel and its content. This interaction fosters a sense of community as viewers feel connected to you as a creator and to each other through shared interests.

D. Content Strategy Insights

- **Performance Analysis:** Analyzing watch time data provides valuable insights into what types of content resonate most with your audience.
- **Content Improvement:** Understanding which videos have higher watch times can help you refine your content strategy, focusing on topics and formats that keep viewers engaged.

3. Strategies to Increase Watch Time

Increasing watch time involves creating engaging content and employing various strategies to keep viewers watching your videos for longer periods. Here are some effective strategies:

A. Create High-Quality Content

- **Value and Relevance:** Ensure your videos provide valuable and relevant information or entertainment to your audience.
- **Production Quality:** Invest in good production quality, including clear audio, high-resolution video, and professional editing.

B. Optimize Video Length

- **Balanced Duration:** Find a balance between video length and content quality. While longer videos can increase watch time, they must remain engaging throughout.

- **Segmenting Content:** For longer videos, segment the content into clear sections with timestamps, making it easier for viewers to navigate.

C. Engage Viewers Early

- **Strong Intro:** Capture viewers' attention within the first few seconds of your video. Use compelling intros, hooks, or teasers to entice viewers to keep watching.
- **Clear Thumbnails and Titles:** Use attractive thumbnails and clear, descriptive titles to set viewer expectations and encourage clicks.

D. Use Playlists Effectively

- **Curated Playlists:** Create playlists that group related videos together. This encourages viewers to watch multiple videos in succession, increasing overall watch time.
- **Auto-Play:** Enable auto-play for your playlists to keep viewers engaged with your content.

E. Utilize End Screens and Cards

- **End Screens:** Use end screens to promote other videos, playlists, or your channel. Encourage viewers to continue watching more of your content.

- **Interactive Cards:** Add interactive cards during your videos to suggest related content and keep viewers engaged.

F. Encourage Viewer Interaction

- **Calls to Action:** Prompt viewers to like, comment, and subscribe. Engaging with your audience can enhance the viewing experience and build loyalty.
- **Q&A Sessions:** Host Q&A sessions or live streams to interact directly with your audience, increasing engagement and watch time.

G. Monitor Analytics and Adjust

- **YouTube Analytics:** Regularly check your YouTube Analytics to understand watch time patterns and identify which videos perform best.
- **Continuous Improvement:** Use the insights gained from analytics to refine your content strategy and improve future videos. YouTube Analytics provides valuable data on viewer demographics, watch time, engagement metrics, and more. By regularly analyzing these metrics, you can identify trends, understand viewer preferences, and pinpoint areas for improvement in your content.

4. Common Pitfalls to Avoid

While focusing on increasing watch time, it's important to avoid common pitfalls that can negatively impact your channel:

A. Clickbait Titles and Thumbnails

- **Misleading Content:** Avoid using misleading titles and thumbnails that do not accurately represent your content. This can lead to viewer dissatisfaction and lower retention rates.
- **Trust Erosion:** Consistently using clickbait can erode trust with your audience, leading to decreased watch time and engagement over time.

B. Overly Long Videos

- **Retention Issues:** Creating excessively long videos without sufficient content value can result in viewers dropping off early, reducing overall watch time.
- **Quality over Quantity:** Focus on quality and relevance rather than just increasing video length for the sake of watch time.

C. Inconsistent Posting Schedule

- **Viewer Expectations:** Inconsistent posting can confuse viewers and reduce engagement. Maintain a regular posting schedule to build and retain your audience.

- **Algorithm Impact:** Irregular uploads can negatively impact your channel's algorithm performance, reducing the chances of your videos being recommended.

5. Examples and Case Studies

Examining examples and case studies can provide valuable insights into how successful creators increase their watch time:

A. Educational Channels

- **In-Depth Tutorials:** Channels that offer in-depth tutorials and educational content often have high watch times. For example, a coding tutorial series that walks viewers through complex topics step-by-step can keep them engaged for extended periods.
- **Interactive Lessons:** Incorporating interactive elements, quizzes, and real-world applications can enhance viewer engagement and retention.

B. Entertainment Channels

- **Storytelling Techniques:** Entertainment channels that use strong storytelling techniques can captivate viewers. For instance, a travel vlogger who shares personal stories, experiences, and tips can keep viewers hooked.

- **Series Format:** Creating a series format with cliffhangers or interconnected episodes encourages viewers to watch multiple videos.

C. Lifestyle and Vlogging Channels

- **Authenticity and Relatability:** Lifestyle and vlogging channels that showcase authentic and relatable content often achieve high watch times. Viewers enjoy following the personal journeys and experiences of creators they connect with.
- **Daily or Weekly Updates:** Regular updates and consistent engagement with viewers help maintain high watch times.

In conclusion, watch time is a critical metric that significantly impacts your YouTube channel's success. By understanding its importance as a key ranking factor in YouTube's algorithm, employing effective strategies to increase it, and avoiding common pitfalls such as clickbait or irrelevant content, you can enhance your content's performance.

Creating engaging videos that capture and maintain viewer interest, optimizing video length to align with audience expectations, and encouraging longer viewing sessions through compelling storytelling or educational content are key tactics.

Strategies to Increase Watch Time

Increasing watch time is essential for the success of your YouTube channel. High watch time not only boosts your visibility on the platform but also enhances viewer engagement and loyalty. Here are detailed strategies to help you increase watch time effectively:

1. Create High-Quality Content

Creating high-quality content is the foundation for increasing watch time. Quality content attracts and retains viewers, encouraging them to watch your videos longer.

A. Provide Value and Relevance

- **Audience Needs:** Understand what your audience wants and create content that addresses their needs, interests, or problems.
- **Unique Value:** Offer unique insights, information, or entertainment that viewers can't find elsewhere.

B. Invest in Production Quality

- **Visual and Audio Quality:** Ensure your videos have high-resolution visuals and clear audio. Poor quality can turn viewers away quickly.

- **Professional Editing:** Use professional editing techniques to make your videos engaging. This includes smooth transitions, appropriate pacing, and eliminating unnecessary parts.

C. Maintain Consistent Quality

- **Content Consistency:** Consistently produce high-quality content to build trust and keep your audience coming back.
- **Brand Identity:** Develop a consistent style and tone that reflects your brand and resonates with your audience.

2. Optimize Video Length

Finding the right balance in video length is crucial. While longer videos can increase watch time, they must remain engaging throughout.

A. Balanced Duration

- **Optimal Length:** Research and determine the optimal length for your content type. For tutorials, 10-20 minutes might be ideal, while vlogs could vary.
- **Content Density:** Ensure that every minute of your video adds value. Avoid filler content that doesn't contribute to the main topic.

B. Segmenting Content

- **Clear Sections:** For longer videos, break your content into clear, logical sections. Use timestamps in the description to help viewers navigate.
- **Mini-Series:** Consider creating a series of shorter videos instead of one long video. This can keep viewers engaged and coming back for more.

3. Engage Viewers Early

Capturing and maintaining viewers' attention in the first few seconds is critical to increasing watch time.

A. Strong Intro

- **Hook:** Start with a compelling hook that grabs attention. This could be an interesting fact, a bold statement, or a preview of what's to come.
- **Value Proposition:** Quickly convey the value or benefit of watching the video. Let viewers know what they will learn or experience.

B. Attractive Thumbnails and Titles

- **Clear Thumbnails:** Use clear, high-quality thumbnails that accurately represent your content and entice clicks.
- **Descriptive Titles:** Craft descriptive and engaging titles that set clear expectations for the viewer.

4. Use Playlists Effectively

Playlists can significantly boost watch time by encouraging viewers to watch multiple videos in succession.

A. Curated Playlists

- **Thematic Grouping:** Group related videos into playlists based on themes, topics, or series. This helps viewers find more content they are interested in.
- **Logical Flow:** Arrange videos in a logical order that makes sense and encourages continuous viewing.

B. Auto-Play

- **Seamless Viewing:** Enable auto-play for playlists to keep viewers watching without interruption. This smooth transition from one video to the next can increase overall watch time.
- **Featured Playlists:** Promote playlists on your channel homepage and within video descriptions to guide viewers to more content. Organizing your videos into thematic playlists helps viewers discover related content and encourages them to engage with multiple videos in one sitting. By curating playlists based on topics, series, or viewer interests, you create a seamless viewing experience that keeps viewers engaged and increases overall watch time.

5. Utilize End Screens and Cards

End screens and cards are powerful tools to promote additional content and keep viewers engaged.

A. End Screens

- **Related Videos:** Use end screens to suggest related videos or playlists. Choose videos that are likely to interest the viewer based on the current video's content.
- **Clear Call to Action:** Include a clear call to action, encouraging viewers to watch the next video or subscribe to your channel.

B. Interactive Cards

- **Relevant Suggestions:** Add interactive cards throughout your video to suggest related content, promote playlists, or link to other resources.
- **Timing:** Place cards at natural break points or during moments when viewers might want additional information. YouTube cards are interactive elements that appear on-screen during a video, allowing you to direct viewers to other videos, playlists, websites, or channels. By strategically placing cards at relevant moments, such as before a key explanation, at the end of a segment, or during a transition, you can enhance viewer engagement and encourage further exploration of your content.

6. Encourage Viewer Interaction

Active engagement with your viewers can enhance the viewing experience and increase watch time.

A. Calls to Action

- **Engagement Prompts:** Prompt viewers to like, comment, and subscribe. Engaging with your audience can foster a sense of community and loyalty.
- **Questions:** Ask questions related to the video content to encourage comments and interaction.

B. Live Streams and Q&A Sessions

- **Direct Interaction:** Host live streams and Q&A sessions to interact directly with your audience. This real-time engagement can boost viewer retention and loyalty.
- **Community Building:** Use these sessions to build a stronger community around your channel, encouraging more frequent and longer viewing. Engage with your audience during live streams by responding to comments, answering questions, and incorporating viewer feedback into your content. This interactive approach not only fosters a sense of connection and belonging among your viewers but also encourages them to return for future live streams and regular uploads.

7. Monitor Analytics and Adjust

Regularly reviewing your YouTube Analytics provides valuable insights into watch time and viewer behavior.

A. YouTube Analytics

- **Watch Time Reports:** Use YouTube Analytics to track watch time, average view duration, and audience retention metrics.
- **Performance Insights:** Identify which videos have the highest watch time and analyze what makes them successful.

B. Continuous Improvement

- **Data-Driven Decisions:** Use the insights gained from analytics to refine your content strategy. Focus on topics and formats that perform well.
- **Experimentation:** Regularly experiment with different content types, lengths, and engagement strategies to see what resonates most with your audience. Test new video formats, such as tutorials, vlogs, or educational content, to gauge viewer interest and engagement levels. Explore varying video lengths to determine optimal durations that maintain viewer attention and encourage longer watch times.

8. Promote Your Videos

Effective promotion can attract more viewers and increase watch time.

A. Social Media

- **Cross-Promotion:** Promote your videos across your social media platforms. Share links, snippets, and highlights to drive traffic to your YouTube channel.
- **Engagement:** Engage with your social media audience to encourage them to watch your videos and share them with their networks.

B. Collaborations

- **Collaborate with Other Creators:** Partner with other YouTubers or influencers to reach a broader audience. Collaborative videos can introduce your content to new viewers and boost watch time.
- **Guest Appearances:** Invite guests to feature in your videos or appear on other channels to expand your reach. Collaborating with other creators, experts, or influencers introduces your channel to their audience, increasing exposure and attracting new viewers who share similar interests. Guest appearances can bring fresh perspectives, expertise, or entertainment value to your content, enhancing its appeal and broadening its appeal.

9. Stay Current with Trends

Keeping up with trends can help you create timely and relevant content that attracts more viewers.

A. Trending Topics

- **Current Events:** Create videos on trending topics, news, or events that are relevant to your niche. Timely content can attract viewers searching for the latest information.
- **Hashtags:** Use trending hashtags in your video descriptions and titles to increase discoverability.

B. Seasonal Content

- **Seasonal Themes:** Create content around holidays, seasons, or special events. Seasonal videos can attract viewers looking for related content during specific times of the year.

10. Utilize SEO Best Practices

Effective search engine optimization (SEO) ensures your videos are discoverable by the right audience.

A. Keyword Research

- **Relevant Keywords:** Conduct keyword research to identify relevant keywords and phrases that potential viewers are searching for.

Incorporate Keywords: Use these keywords in your video titles, descriptions, and tags to improve search visibility.

B. Metadata Optimization

- **Accurate Descriptions:** Write detailed and accurate video descriptions that include relevant keywords and provide a clear summary of the content.
- **Consistent Tagging:** Use consistent and relevant tags across your videos to help YouTube's algorithm understand your content better.

In conclusion, increasing watch time on YouTube requires a combination of high-quality content, strategic engagement techniques, effective use of YouTube's features, and continuous analysis and improvement. By implementing these strategies, you can enhance your content's performance, attract more viewers, and foster long-term growth and success for your channel. Moreover, experimenting with different content formats, collaborating with others, and adapting to audience preferences ensures that your channel remains dynamic and relevant. Continuous analysis of performance metrics allows you to refine your strategies and improve content delivery over time.

Analyzing Audience Retention Metrics

Analyzing audience retention metrics is crucial for understanding how viewers interact with your content and identifying areas for improvement. Audience retention refers to the percentage of a video that viewers watch and provides insights into the parts of your video that are most engaging or where viewers tend to drop off.

Key Aspects of Analyzing Audience Retention Metrics

1. Overall Retention Rate:

This metric shows the average percentage of a video that viewers watch. A higher retention rate indicates that viewers find your content engaging and are watching most of it. Aim for a high overall retention rate to ensure your videos are captivating and maintaining viewer interest.

2. Retention Graph:

The retention graph provides a visual representation of viewer engagement throughout the video. It shows where viewers are dropping off, rewatching, or skipping parts of the video. Analyzing this graph helps you identify specific segments that either captivate or lose your audience.

3. Key Moments for Audience Retention:

- **Intro:** The first 15-30 seconds are crucial. If viewers drop off quickly, it may indicate that your intro needs to be more engaging.
- **Peaks:** Peaks in the retention graph indicate moments where viewers rewatch sections, suggesting these parts are particularly interesting or valuable.
- **Valleys:** Valleys or sharp drops signify points where viewers lose interest and leave the video. Identifying and improving these segments can help maintain viewer attention.

4. Segment Analysis:

Break down your video into segments (intro, main content, conclusion) and analyze retention for each part. This helps you understand which sections are performing well and which need improvement.

5. Comparing Videos:

Compare retention metrics across different videos to identify patterns and trends. Determine what works well and apply those insights to future content. For instance, if videos with certain formats or topics consistently have higher retention, consider focusing more on those.

6. Audience Demographics:

Examine retention metrics across different demographic groups (age, gender, location) to understand how various segments of your audience engage with your content. Tailoring content to the preferences of your most engaged demographics can boost overall retention.

7. Annotations and End Screens:

Analyze how viewers interact with annotations, end screens, and other interactive elements. Effective use of these tools can keep viewers engaged and encourage them to watch more of your content.

Tips for Improving Audience Retention

1. Hook Viewers Early:

Start your videos with a strong hook that grabs attention within the first few seconds. Clearly state what the video is about and why viewers should keep watching.

2. Maintain a Good Pace:

Keep your content well-paced and avoid long, drawn-out sections. Editing out unnecessary parts can help maintain viewer interest.

3. Use Visuals and Engagement:

Incorporate visuals, animations, and on-screen text to make your content more dynamic. Ask questions, use humor, and vary your delivery to keep viewers engaged.

4. Summarize and Preview:

Summarize key points and preview what's coming next to keep viewers intrigued. This can encourage them to stick around to see the full content.

5. Call to Actions:

Use strategic calls to action (CTAs) throughout your video to encourage viewers to like, comment, and subscribe. Engaging with viewers through CTAs can keep them more involved with your content.

By regularly analyzing audience retention metrics and implementing these strategies, you can create more engaging content that keeps viewers watching longer, enhances their experience, and contributes to the growth and success of your YouTube channel. By understanding which parts of your videos captivate or lose viewers, you can tailor your content to better meet their expectations and preferences.

Chapter 6
Enhancing Viewer Engagement

Encouraging Likes, Comments, and Shares

Encouraging likes, comments, and shares is essential for increasing engagement on your YouTube channel. These interactions signal to YouTube that your content is valuable, which can improve your video's ranking in search results and recommendations, leading to greater visibility and growth. Here are some strategies to effectively encourage your audience to like, comment, and share your videos:

Encouraging Likes

1. Ask Directly:

Don't hesitate to ask your viewers to like the video. A simple request at the beginning, middle, or end of the video can remind viewers to show their appreciation if they enjoyed the content.

2. Explain the Benefits:

Briefly explain how liking the video helps the channel grow. Viewers are more likely to engage if they understand the positive impact their like has on your channel.

3. Set Like Goals:

Set a like goal for your video and communicate it to your viewers. This can create a sense of community effort and motivate viewers to contribute to reaching the goal.

Encouraging Comments

1. Ask Open-Ended Questions:

Pose questions related to your video's content. Open-ended questions invite viewers to share their opinions, experiences, and thoughts, leading to more comments.

2. Respond to Comments:

Engage with your audience by responding to their comments. This shows that you value their input and encourages more viewers to join the conversation.

3. Create Discussion Points:

Include discussion points in your videos that prompt viewers to comment. For example, ask for feedback on a specific topic, suggestions for future content, or their favorite part of the video.

4. Highlight Viewer Comments:

Feature viewer comments in your videos or give shout-outs to those who leave thoughtful comments. This recognition can encourage more viewers to participate in the comment section.

Encouraging Shares

1. Remind Viewers to Share:

Regularly remind your viewers to share your video with friends and on social media if they found it valuable or entertaining. A direct request can increase the likelihood of shares.

2. Create Shareable Content:

Focus on creating content that viewers will naturally want to share, such as informative tutorials, entertaining stories, or inspirational messages. High-quality, shareable content is more likely to be passed on.

3. Utilize Social Media:

Promote your videos on your social media platforms and encourage your followers to share them. Include social media sharing buttons in your video descriptions to make it easy for viewers to share.

4. Collaborate with Other Creators:

Collaborate with other YouTubers or influencers in your niche. When they share the collaborative content with their audience, it increases the chances of your video being shared more widely.

Creating a Community Atmosphere

1. Foster a Sense of Belonging:

Create a welcoming and inclusive environment where viewers feel like they are part of a community. Address your audience as a group and refer to them collectively to strengthen the community feel.

2. Regular Updates and Engagement:

Keep your audience updated with regular content and engage with them through community posts, live streams, and Q&A sessions. Consistent interaction helps build a loyal and engaged viewer base.

3. Exclusive Content and Incentives:

Offer exclusive content, behind-the-scenes access, or special incentives for those who engage the most. This could include giveaways, special shout-outs, or access to members-only content.

By implementing these strategies, you can create an engaging environment that encourages your viewers to like, comment, and share your content. Asking viewers directly to like your videos, explaining the benefits of their likes, and setting achievable like goals can significantly increase the number of likes your videos receive. Engaging with your audience by responding to comments and asking open-ended questions not only encourages more comments but also creates a lively discussion around your content.

Encouraging shares involves creating content that viewers find valuable and naturally want to share. Reminding viewers to share your videos, utilizing social media platforms to promote your content, and collaborating with other creators can extend your reach and attract new viewers. Creating shareable content, such as tutorials, stories, or inspirational messages, ensures that your videos have a broader appeal and are more likely to be shared.

Fostering a sense of community is essential for building a loyal viewer base. Creating a welcoming atmosphere, regularly engaging with your audience through updates and live streams, and offering exclusive content or incentives for engagement can strengthen the connection between you and your viewers.

Effective Use of Calls to Action (CTAs)

Effective use of calls to action (CTAs) is vital for driving viewer engagement and achieving your goals on YouTube. CTAs guide your audience on what to do next, whether it's subscribing to your channel, liking your video, commenting, sharing, or visiting a link. Here's how to effectively incorporate CTAs into your videos:

Strategically Placing CTAs

1. Introduction:

Include a brief CTA at the beginning of your video. This could be a quick reminder to subscribe to your channel or to like the video if they find it useful. By placing a CTA early, you catch viewers before they potentially drop off.

2. Throughout the Video:

Integrate CTAs naturally within the content. For example, if you're discussing a specific topic, you might prompt viewers to comment with their opinions or questions. Mid-video CTAs can be less intrusive and blend seamlessly into your narrative.

3. End of the Video:

Conclude with a strong CTA. Encourage viewers to like, comment, and subscribe, and guide them on what to watch next by suggesting other videos or playlists. This is also an ideal place to promote external links, such as your website, social media, or merchandise.

Types of CTAs and Their Uses

1. Engagement CTAs:

- **Like and Subscribe:** Directly ask viewers to like the video and subscribe to your channel. Explain how these actions support your content creation.
- **Comments:** Encourage viewers to leave comments by asking specific questions or seeking feedback. This not only increases engagement but also provides valuable insights into your audience's preferences.

2. Sharing and Social Media CTAs:

- **Share the Video:** Prompt viewers to share your video with friends or on their social media platforms. Explain the value of spreading your content to a wider audience.

- **Follow on Social Media:** Encourage viewers to follow you on other social media platforms for additional content and updates. Use visual and verbal cues to make it easy for them to find you.

3. Content-Specific CTAs:

- **Watch More:** Direct viewers to watch more of your content by linking related videos or playlists. This keeps viewers on your channel longer and increases watch time.
- **Join Mailing List:** If you have a newsletter or mailing list, ask viewers to sign up for exclusive content, updates, or special offers. Provide a clear and easy way to subscribe.

Making CTAs Engaging and Effective

1. Be Clear and Concise:

Ensure your CTAs are straightforward and easy to understand. Avoid overly complex instructions that might confuse viewers. A clear CTA is more likely to be followed.

2. Use Visual Cues:

Enhance your verbal CTAs with visual elements, such as text overlays, animations, or end screens. Visual cues help reinforce the action you want viewers to take and make the CTA more noticeable.

3. Create a Sense of Urgency:

Encourage immediate action by creating a sense of urgency. Use phrases like "Subscribe now," "Leave a comment below," or "Don't miss out." This can motivate viewers to take action promptly.

4. Offer Incentives:

Provide incentives for following your CTAs. This could be a giveaway, access to exclusive content, or a shout-out in a future video. Incentives can significantly boost engagement rates.

5. Personalize Your CTAs:

Tailor your CTAs to fit the content and context of each video. A personalized CTA feels more relevant and compelling to the viewer, increasing the likelihood of action.

Tracking and Optimizing CTAs

1. Monitor Engagement:

Track the performance of your CTAs by monitoring engagement metrics such as likes, comments, shares, and subscriptions. Analyzing this data helps you understand which CTAs are most effective.

2. Experiment and Adapt:

Don't be afraid to experiment with different types of CTAs, placements, and wording. A/B testing can help identify what resonates best with your audience. Adapt your strategy based on what works.

3. Feedback Loop:

Use feedback from your audience to refine your CTAs. Pay attention to comments and engagement patterns to better understand viewer preferences and behavior. By effectively utilizing CTAs, you can guide your viewers to take desired actions that support your channel's growth and engagement. Whether it's liking a video, subscribing to your channel, or sharing your content, well-crafted CTAs can significantly enhance viewer interaction and contribute to the overall success of your YouTube channel.

These actions not only boost your engagement metrics but also signal to YouTube's algorithm that your content is valuable, which can lead to higher rankings in search results and recommendations. Additionally, effective CTAs help build a sense of community among your viewers. Encouraging comments and feedback fosters a two-way conversation, making your audience feel more connected to you and your content.

Creating Interactive Content

Creating interactive content is a powerful way to engage your audience and make your videos more dynamic and memorable. Interactive content encourages viewers to participate actively rather than passively consuming information, which can lead to higher engagement rates, increased watch time, and stronger viewer loyalty. Here's how you can create interactive content for your YouTube channel:

Types of Interactive Content

1. Quizzes and Polls:

- **YouTube Polls:** Use YouTube's community tab to create polls that engage your audience with questions about their preferences, opinions, or future content ideas. Polls are a simple yet effective way to interact with your viewers.
- **In-Video Quizzes:** Incorporate quizzes within your videos using YouTube cards or third-party tools. Ask questions related to the video's content and provide multiple-choice answers, encouraging viewers to participate and test their knowledge.

2. Interactive Stories:

- **Choose-Your-Own-Adventure:** Create a series of videos where viewers can choose the direction of the story by clicking on different video links. This type of interactive storytelling keeps viewers engaged as they control the narrative.
- **Viewer Suggestions:** Develop stories or content ideas based on viewer suggestions. Ask your audience for input and incorporate their ideas into your videos, making them feel involved in the creative process.

3. Live Streams and Q&A Sessions:

- **Live Chats:** Host live streams where viewers can interact with you in real-time through the chat feature. Answer their questions, respond to comments, and acknowledge their participation to foster a sense of community.
- **Q&A Sessions:** Dedicate live streams or video segments to answering viewer questions. Encourage viewers to submit questions beforehand or during the live session, and address them directly in your video.

4. Interactive Tutorials and Challenges:

- **Step-by-Step Guides:** Create tutorials that involve viewers actively following along. Use on-screen prompts to guide them through each step and encourage them to pause the video and try the steps themselves.
- **Challenges:** Introduce challenges that viewers can participate in and share their results. This could be anything from a fitness challenge to a cooking recipe. Ask viewers to share their experiences in the comments or on social media.

Tools and Techniques for Interactive Content

1. YouTube Cards and End Screens:

Use YouTube cards to add interactive elements like polls, links to other videos, or prompts to subscribe. End screens can also direct viewers to related content, encouraging further interaction.

2. Annotations and Overlays:

Although YouTube annotations have been discontinued, you can use text overlays and graphics within your video editing software to create interactive elements. Highlight key points, add prompts, or display questions that viewers can answer in the comments.

3. Interactive Video Platforms:

Consider using platforms like H5P or Eko to create highly interactive video content. These tools offer advanced features like branching scenarios, interactive quizzes, and clickable hotspots.

Benefits of Interactive Content

1. Increased Engagement:

Interactive content naturally encourages viewers to engage more deeply with your videos. This increased engagement can lead to longer watch times, higher retention rates, and more interactions such as likes, comments, and shares.

2. Enhanced Learning and Retention:

For educational content, interactivity helps reinforce learning by actively involving viewers in the process. Quizzes, challenges, and hands-on tutorials can make information more memorable and impactful.

3. Stronger Community and Loyalty:

Interactive content fosters a sense of community by making viewers feel like active participants rather than passive observers. Engaging with your audience in real-time through live streams or incorporating their suggestions into your content can build stronger viewer loyalty.

4. Better Feedback and Insights:

Interactive elements like polls and Q&A sessions provide valuable feedback from your audience. This direct input can help you tailor your content to better meet viewer preferences and improve your overall channel strategy.

Tips for Creating Effective Interactive Content

1. Plan and Script:

Plan your interactive elements carefully and integrate them naturally into your video script. Ensure that they add value and enhance the viewer experience rather than feeling forced or gimmicky.

2. Keep it Simple:

While interactivity can be exciting, it's important to keep it simple and intuitive. Overcomplicating interactive elements can confuse viewers and detract from the overall experience.

3. Promote Participation:

Encourage viewers to participate by clearly explaining how they can engage with the interactive elements. Use verbal prompts, visual cues, and clear instructions to guide them.

4. Analyze Results:

After publishing interactive content, analyze engagement metrics to understand what worked and what didn't. Use this data to refine your approach and create even more effective interactive videos in the future.

By incorporating interactive content into your YouTube strategy, you can create a more engaging and dynamic experience for your viewers. This approach not only enhances viewer satisfaction but also strengthens your connection with your audience, driving long-term success for your channel.

Interactive content encourages active participation, making viewers feel more involved and valued. As a result, they are more likely to return, engage with future content, and become loyal supporters.

Additionally, interactive content can set your channel apart in a crowded digital landscape. By offering unique and immersive experiences, you can attract new viewers who are looking for something different and memorable. This differentiation can lead to increased subscriber growth and higher overall channel engagement.

Chapter 7
The Importance of Consistency

Developing a Consistent Upload Schedule

Developing a consistent upload schedule is crucial for the success of your YouTube channel. A regular posting routine helps build anticipation among your audience, improves viewer retention, and can positively impact your channel's performance in YouTube's algorithm. Here's a detailed guide on how to create and maintain a consistent upload schedule:

Benefits of a Consistent Upload Schedule

1. Builds Audience Expectations:

Regular uploads help your audience know when to expect new content. This predictability can build anticipation and loyalty, as viewers are more likely to return to your channel if they know when new videos will be available.

2. Improves Viewer Retention:

Consistency in your upload schedule can lead to better viewer retention. When viewers consistently find valuable content on your channel, they are more likely to stay engaged and watch your videos regularly.

3. Enhances Algorithm Performance:

YouTube's algorithm favors channels that upload regularly. Consistent uploads can lead to improved visibility in search results and recommendations, driving more traffic to your channel.

4. Establishes a Routine for Content Creation:

A set schedule helps you plan and manage your content creation process more effectively. It encourages discipline and ensures that you are producing content consistently, which is vital for long-term growth.

Steps to Develop a Consistent Upload Schedule

1. Determine Your Capacity:

Assess how much time you can realistically dedicate to creating, editing, and publishing videos. Consider your other commitments and be honest about how many videos you can produce without compromising quality.

2. Choose Your Frequency:

Decide how often you want to upload videos. Common frequencies include once a week, twice a week, or even daily. The key is to choose a frequency that you can maintain consistently.

3. Select Specific Days and Times:

Pick specific days and times to upload your videos. Consistency in timing helps your audience know exactly when to expect new content. Analyze your audience's activity patterns to determine the best times for uploads.

4. Plan Your Content Calendar:

Create a content calendar to plan your videos in advance. Outline the topics, titles, and key points for each video. Planning ahead reduces the stress of last-minute content creation and ensures a steady flow of videos.

Tips for Maintaining a Consistent Schedule

1. Batch Production:

Consider batch producing your content. Filming and editing multiple videos in one session can save time and provide a buffer, ensuring you have videos ready to go even during busy periods.

2. Use Scheduling Tools:

Utilize YouTube's scheduling feature to upload and schedule videos in advance. This ensures that your videos go live at the designated time, even if you're not available to upload them manually.

3. Stay Flexible and Adapt:

While consistency is important, it's also essential to remain flexible. Life events or unexpected circumstances may disrupt your schedule. Communicate any changes to your audience and get back on track as soon as possible.

4. Monitor Performance and Adjust:

Regularly review your analytics to understand how your schedule impacts your channel's performance. If you notice certain days or times perform better, consider adjusting your schedule accordingly.

5. Communicate with Your Audience:

Keep your audience informed about your upload schedule. Mention it in your videos, include it in your channel description, and remind viewers of upcoming content. Transparency builds trust and sets clear expectations.

Dealing with Challenges

1. Managing Burnout:

Avoid overcommitting yourself. Consistency doesn't mean you have to produce an overwhelming amount of content.

Focus on quality over quantity and give yourself time to rest and recharge.

2. Handling Creative Blocks:

Creative blocks are natural. Overcome them by seeking inspiration from other creators, exploring new content formats, or taking breaks to refresh your mind. Having a content calendar can also help mitigate creative blocks by providing a clear direction.

3. Balancing Quality and Quantity:

While maintaining a regular upload schedule is important, don't sacrifice quality for the sake of consistency. Strive to deliver high-quality content that provides value to your audience, even if it means uploading less frequently.

Leveraging Analytics for Improvement

1. Analyze Viewer Behavior:

Use YouTube Analytics to understand viewer behavior and preferences. Look at metrics such as watch time, audience retention, and engagement rates to determine the effectiveness of your schedule.

2. Experiment and Optimize:

Don't be afraid to experiment with different upload times or frequencies. Monitor the results and optimize your schedule based on what works best for your audience and channel performance.

3. Feedback Loop:

Solicit feedback from your viewers. Ask them about their preferred upload times and types of content they enjoy. Incorporating viewer feedback can help you refine your schedule and content strategy.

By developing and maintaining a consistent upload schedule, you can enhance viewer engagement, build a loyal audience, and improve your channel's performance on YouTube. Consistency, combined with quality content, creates a strong foundation for sustained growth and success.

Viewers appreciate knowing when they can expect new videos, which fosters a habit of returning to your channel regularly. This regularity not only boosts your watch time and engagement metrics but also strengthens the bond between you and your audience.

Benefits of Consistency for Algorithm Performance

Maintaining a consistent upload schedule on YouTube can significantly enhance your channel's performance in terms of visibility, engagement, and growth. The platform's algorithm favors regular and reliable content creators, which can lead to numerous benefits. Here's an in-depth look at how consistency positively impacts YouTube's algorithm and your channel's success:

Improved Search Rankings

1. Higher Frequency of Uploads:

Regular uploads increase the chances of your videos being indexed by YouTube's search engine. More frequent content updates mean that you have more opportunities to appear in search results, which can lead to increased visibility and discoverability.

2. Algorithmic Favorability:

YouTube's algorithm tends to favor channels that upload consistently. The algorithm prioritizes active channels, assuming that consistent uploads indicate an active and engaged creator.

Enhanced Viewer Engagement Metrics

1. Increased Watch Time:

Consistent uploads encourage viewers to spend more time on your channel. As viewers anticipate and regularly watch your new videos, overall watch time increases. Since watch time is a crucial metric for the algorithm, higher watch time can significantly boost your channel's visibility.

2. Improved Audience Retention:

Regular content releases can help maintain and improve audience retention. Viewers are more likely to stay engaged and watch more of your videos when they know you post regularly. Higher audience retention signals to the algorithm that your content is engaging and valuable.

Stronger Subscriber Growth

1. Building Viewer Habits:

When viewers know you upload on specific days, they are more likely to return to your channel regularly. This habit formation can lead to increased subscriber growth as viewers appreciate the reliability and predictability of your content schedule.

2. Encouraging Subscriptions:

Consistent uploads make it more compelling for viewers to subscribe. Knowing that they won't miss out on regular content, viewers are more likely to hit the subscribe button to stay updated with your channel's latest offerings.

Increased Recommendations and Suggested Videos

1. Higher Likelihood of Recommendations:

Channels that upload consistently are more likely to have their videos recommended by YouTube. The algorithm promotes content from active creators, which means your videos are more likely to appear in the "Up Next" section and on viewers' homepages.

2. Improved Suggested Video Placements:

Consistent upload schedules can lead to your videos being suggested alongside other popular content. When the algorithm recognizes that your channel regularly provides fresh content, it is more likely to include your videos in the suggested video feed of users who have shown interest in similar content.

Better Analytics and Data Insights

1. Reliable Performance Metrics:

Consistent uploads provide a steady stream of data, allowing you to track performance metrics more accurately. Regular data points make it easier to identify trends, understand viewer behavior, and make informed decisions about your content strategy.

2. Enhanced A/B Testing:

With a regular upload schedule, you can experiment with different types of content, thumbnails, titles, and descriptions. Consistency allows for more effective A/B testing, helping you determine what works best for your audience and optimizing your content accordingly.

Strengthened Channel Authority and Credibility

1. Building Authority:

A consistent upload schedule helps establish your channel as a reliable source of content. Over time, this builds your authority in your niche or industry, attracting more viewers who trust your expertise and insights.

2. Increased Credibility:

Regular uploads demonstrate commitment and professionalism, which can enhance your credibility with both viewers and potential collaborators. Brands and sponsors are more likely to partner with creators who have a proven track record of consistent content production.

Long-Term Growth and Sustainability

1. Sustainable Growth:

Consistency in uploads leads to sustainable channel growth. As you continue to provide valuable content on a regular basis, your audience grows steadily, and engagement metrics improve, creating a positive feedback loop that supports long-term success.

2. Resilience Against Algorithm Changes:

YouTube's algorithm frequently changes, but maintaining a consistent upload schedule can help mitigate the impact of these changes. Regular content production ensures that your channel remains active and adaptable to algorithmic shifts, maintaining visibility and engagement.

In summary, developing and maintaining a consistent upload schedule is crucial for leveraging YouTube's algorithm to your advantage. Consistency not only boosts search rankings by increasing the frequency of your content appearing in search results but also enhances viewer engagement metrics such as watch time and audience retention. This, in turn, signals to YouTube that your content is valuable and encourages the platform to recommend your videos to a broader audience.

Moreover, a consistent upload schedule fosters subscriber growth as viewers are more likely to subscribe when they know they can expect regular updates from your channel. This steady growth in subscribers strengthens your channel's community and increases the potential reach of each new video. As your audience grows and engages more consistently with your content, YouTube's algorithm is further incentivized to promote your videos through suggested video placements and recommendations.

Ultimately, these cumulative benefits create a positive cycle of growth and visibility on YouTube, setting the stage for sustained success over the long term. By adhering to a consistent upload schedule and consistently delivering high-quality content, you enhance your channel's credibility, authority, and appeal to both viewers and the platform itself.

Managing Content Calendars

Managing a content calendar is essential for organizing and optimizing your YouTube channel's content strategy. A well-structured content calendar helps you plan, create, and distribute videos effectively, ensuring consistency and alignment with your audience's interests. Here's how to effectively manage your content calendar for YouTube:

Establishing Goals and Themes

1. Define Your Objectives:

Begin by outlining your channel's goals and objectives. Determine what you aim to achieve with your content, whether it's increasing subscribers, improving engagement, or promoting products/services. These goals will guide your content planning and scheduling decisions.

2. Identify Content Themes:

Develop overarching themes or topics that resonate with your target audience. Consider the types of content that perform well on your channel and align with your niche or expertise. Having predefined themes makes it easier to brainstorm ideas and maintain consistency in your content offerings.

Planning and Scheduling

1. Create a Content Calendar Template:

Use a spreadsheet or online tool to create a content calendar template. Include columns for video titles, publish dates, planned release times, content type, keywords/tags, and any relevant notes. This template serves as a centralized hub for organizing your content ideas and scheduling uploads.

2. Set a Posting Schedule:

Determine how frequently you will upload videos (e.g., weekly, bi-weekly) and establish specific days and times for publication. Consistency is key, as it helps build viewer expectations and improves your channel's performance in YouTube's algorithm.

3. Plan Ahead:

By having a content calendar, you can strategically align your videos with key dates, holidays, or events relevant to your audience. Additionally, planning ahead allows for better collaboration with team members, sponsors, or influencers, ensuring everyone is on the same page and contributing effectively. Consistent and well-timed content helps in building and retaining a loyal audience, ultimately leading to sustained growth and engagement on your platform.

Content Creation and Production

1. Batch Production:

Consider batch producing multiple videos in one session. This approach can streamline your workflow and increase efficiency. Batch filming and editing sessions allow you to create a backlog of content, which is useful for maintaining consistency during busy periods.

2. Collaborate and Outsource:

Collaborate with other creators or delegate tasks to freelancers or team members if necessary. Outsourcing certain aspects of content creation, such as editing or graphic design, can help you focus on core tasks and adhere to your content calendar.

Optimization and Distribution

1. Optimize Video SEO:

Before publishing, optimize each video for search engines (SEO). Use relevant keywords in titles, descriptions, and tags to improve discoverability. Consider how each video fits into your overall content strategy and its potential impact on viewer engagement.

2. Leverage Scheduling Tools:

Use YouTube's scheduling feature to set publish dates and times for your videos in advance. This ensures that your content goes live at optimal times for your audience, even if you are unavailable to manually publish.

Monitoring and Adjustments

1. Track Performance Metrics:

Regularly monitor key performance metrics such as watch time, views, engagement rate, and subscriber growth. Analyze how each video performs against your goals and adjust your content strategy accordingly.

2. Incorporate Viewer Feedback:

Engaging with your audience through comments and feedback not only builds a sense of community but also provides invaluable insights into their preferences and interests. Analyzing analytics data helps identify patterns in viewer behavior, such as peak viewing times and popular content formats. By leveraging this data, you can make informed decisions about the types of content to produce and the best times to release them.

2. Stay Flexible and Adapt:

Remain flexible and open to adjusting your content calendar based on evolving trends, seasonal topics, or unexpected opportunities. Flexibility allows you to capitalize on new content ideas and maintain engagement with your audience.

A well-managed content calendar is a cornerstone of a successful YouTube channel. By strategically planning, scheduling, and optimizing your content, you can maintain consistency, enhance viewer engagement, and drive long-term growth. Effective content calendar management not only streamlines your workflow but also ensures that your videos are aligned with your audience's interests and preferences, ultimately contributing to the overall success and sustainability of your YouTube presence.

Moreover, incorporating a feedback loop into your content calendar can significantly enhance your content's quality and relevance. Regularly reviewing and assessing the performance of your videos allows you to pinpoint successful elements and areas needing improvement. By actively seeking and integrating viewer suggestions and critiques, you can foster a more engaged and loyal community. This iterative process ensures your content remains dynamic and adaptable, catering to evolving viewer preferences and trends.

Chapter 8
Leveraging Playlists and Series

Creating Playlists to Boost Watch Time

Creating playlists is a strategic way to boost watch time on your YouTube channel. Playlists organize your content into cohesive, easily navigable collections, encouraging viewers to watch multiple videos in one session. This not only improves individual video performance but also enhances overall channel metrics. Here's a comprehensive guide on how to effectively use playlists to increase watch time:

Benefits of Using Playlists

1. Enhanced Viewer Experience:

Playlists provide a seamless viewing experience by automatically playing the next video in the sequence. This reduces the likelihood of viewers navigating away from your channel after watching a single video.

2. Increased Watch Time:

By grouping related videos, playlists encourage viewers to watch more content consecutively, thereby increasing total watch time.

Longer watch times signal to YouTube's algorithm that your content is engaging, potentially improving your channel's visibility and recommendations.

3. Improved Content Discoverability:

Playlists can help new viewers discover more of your content. When they find one video interesting, a playlist format makes it easy for them to continue watching related videos without searching for them individually.

4. Better Organization:

Playlists organize your content into thematic or chronological collections, making it easier for viewers to find specific types of videos. This structured approach can attract more subscribers who appreciate the curated viewing experience.

Steps to Create Effective Playlists

1. Identify Themes and Series:

Group your videos by themes, topics, or series. For example, if you have a cooking channel, create playlists for different types of cuisine, cooking techniques, or meal prep series. This thematic organization helps viewers find content that interests them and keeps them engaged for longer.

2. Curate and Sequence Videos:

Carefully curate and sequence the videos within each playlist. Start with an introductory video that captures interest and logically progress through related content. Ensure that each video naturally leads to the next to maintain viewer engagement.

3. Optimize Playlist Titles and Descriptions:

Use clear, descriptive titles for your playlists that include relevant keywords. This improves SEO and helps viewers understand what to expect. Additionally, write detailed descriptions that outline the content of the playlist and include keywords to improve discoverability.

4. Use Engaging Thumbnails:

Consistent and visually appealing thumbnails across your playlist can entice viewers to watch more videos. Ensure thumbnails are relevant to the content and maintain a cohesive style that represents your channel's brand.

Advanced Playlist Strategies

1. Create Multi-Video Tutorials:

For educational or instructional content, create playlists that guide viewers through a step-by-step process.

Each video can cover a specific part of the tutorial, encouraging viewers to watch the entire series to gain full understanding.

2. Feature Playlists on Your Channel Page:

Highlight important playlists on your channel's homepage. Use sections to showcase different playlists prominently, making it easier for visitors to find and start watching multiple videos from your collection.

3. Cross-Promote Playlists:

Promote your playlists in your video descriptions, end screens, and cards. Encourage viewers to check out the playlist for more related content. Verbal mentions within the videos can also prompt viewers to explore the playlists.

4. Collaborate with Other Creators:

Collaborate with other YouTubers to create joint playlists that feature videos from both channels. This can introduce your content to a wider audience and drive more traffic and watch time.

5. Analyze Playlist Performance:

Use YouTube Analytics to track the performance of your playlists.

Monitor metrics such as average view duration, watch time, and viewer drop-off points. Use these insights to refine your playlist strategy and improve viewer retention.

Tips for Maintaining and Updating Playlists

1. Regularly Update Playlists:

Keep your playlists fresh by regularly adding new videos. Update older playlists with recent content to maintain relevance and encourage viewers to revisit them.

2. Remove Underperforming Videos:

If certain videos within a playlist are underperforming, consider removing or replacing them. Focus on curating high-performing content that maintains viewer interest throughout the playlist.

3. Create Seasonal or Topical Playlists:

Develop playlists around seasonal events, holidays, or trending topics. These playlists can attract viewers searching for specific content during particular times of the year.

4. Encourage Viewer Feedback:

Solicit feedback from your audience about your playlists. Ask for suggestions on content they would like to see grouped together or ideas for new playlists. This engagement can provide valuable insights and strengthen your connection with viewers.

Creating and managing playlists effectively can significantly boost watch time on your YouTube channel. By organizing your content into well-structured, thematic collections, you enhance the viewer experience, encourage longer viewing sessions, and improve your channel's performance in YouTube's algorithm. Implement these strategies to leverage playlists as a powerful tool for driving engagement, increasing watch time, and achieving long-term success on YouTube.

Playlists not only keep viewers engaged by automatically playing the next video, but they also help new audiences discover more of your content without having to search for it. This seamless experience keeps viewers on your channel longer, which boosts overall watch time and signals to YouTube's algorithm that your content is valuable and worth recommending. Furthermore, well-crafted playlists can act as a guide for viewers, making it easier for them to navigate through related topics or series.

Structuring Video Series for Maximum Impact

Creating a well-structured video series is a powerful way to engage your audience and keep them coming back for more. A series can help establish a deeper connection with viewers, provide valuable content in a digestible format, and significantly boost your channel's watch time and subscriber growth. Here's a comprehensive guide on structuring your video series for maximum impact:

Identifying the Right Topic and Format

1. Choose a Relevant Topic:

Select a topic that aligns with your channel's niche and audience interests. The topic should be broad enough to allow multiple episodes but focused enough to maintain viewer interest. Research trending topics, audience feedback, and competitor content to identify potential series ideas.

2. Determine the Series Format:

Decide on the format that best suits your content and audience. Options include tutorials, storytelling, interviews, product reviews, or a combination of formats.

The format should enhance the content and make it easier for viewers to follow along.

Planning and Pre-Production

1. Outline the Series Structure:

Create a detailed outline for the entire series. Plan the number of episodes, key points to cover in each episode, and the overall narrative or progression. This ensures a cohesive and logical flow throughout the series.

2. Script and Storyboard:

Write scripts or detailed outlines for each episode. Consider creating storyboards to visualize the content and ensure consistency in style and presentation. This preparation helps maintain focus and clarity in each video.

3. Plan for Cliffhangers and Teasers:

Incorporate cliffhangers or teasers at the end of each episode to encourage viewers to watch the next installment. This technique keeps the audience engaged and eagerly anticipating the next video.

Production and Content Creation

1. Maintain Consistent Quality:

Ensure that each episode maintains a consistent level of quality in terms of production values, audio, and visuals. Consistency builds trust and keeps viewers invested in the series.

2. Record in Batches:

Consider batch recording multiple episodes in one session. This approach can save time and ensure continuity in terms of setting, wardrobe, and energy levels. Batch recording also helps in maintaining a regular upload schedule.

3. Engage Viewers Throughout:

Keep your audience engaged by asking questions, encouraging comments, and addressing viewer feedback in subsequent episodes. This interaction fosters a sense of community and investment in the series.

Post-Production and Optimization

1. Edit for Consistency:

Edit each episode to ensure a consistent pace, style, and tone. Use similar transitions, graphics, and music to create a cohesive viewing experience.

2. Optimize for SEO:

Use relevant keywords in titles, descriptions, and tags to improve discoverability. Create custom thumbnails for each episode that follow a consistent theme, making it easy for viewers to recognize the series.

3. Add Playlists and End Screens:

Organize the series into a dedicated playlist to facilitate easy navigation and continuous viewing. Use end screens and cards to direct viewers to the next episode or related content, enhancing watch time.

Promotion and Engagement

1. Promote Across Platforms:

Announce the series on your social media channels, website, and email newsletters. Share teasers or trailers to generate excitement and anticipation. Cross-promotion helps attract new viewers and retain existing ones.

2. Engage with Your Audience:

Actively engage with viewers by responding to comments and encouraging discussions. Create a sense of community around the series, which can lead to higher viewer retention and loyalty.

3. Collaborate with Other Creators:

Collaborate with other YouTubers or influencers to expand your reach. Featuring guest appearances or co-hosting episodes can attract new audiences and provide fresh perspectives.

Monitoring and Adjusting

1. Track Performance Metrics:

Use YouTube Analytics to monitor key metrics such as watch time, retention rates, and viewer feedback. Analyze the data to identify strengths and areas for improvement.

2. Adapt Based on Feedback:

Be open to making adjustments based on viewer feedback and performance data. If certain episodes perform better, analyze why and incorporate those elements into future episodes.

3. Plan Future Series:

Based on the success and learnings from your current series, plan future series to continue engaging your audience. Continuously innovate and refine your approach to keep content fresh and exciting.

Structuring a video series effectively involves careful planning, consistent production quality, and active engagement with your audience. By choosing relevant topics, maintaining a cohesive narrative, and optimizing each episode for discoverability and engagement, you can create compelling series that captivate viewers and drive long-term success for your YouTube channel. Implement these strategies to leverage the power of video series, boost watch time, and build a loyal community of subscribers.

When executed well, a video series can become a cornerstone of your content strategy, offering viewers a reason to return to your channel regularly. The anticipation built through cliffhangers and teasers keeps your audience hooked, while interactive elements like Q&A sessions or viewer polls foster a sense of community and involvement. This not only enhances viewer retention but also encourages viewers to share your content, expanding your reach organically.

Moreover, a structured series allows you to delve deeper into topics, providing comprehensive coverage that single videos often can't achieve. This depth of content positions you as an authority in your niche, attracting viewers who seek in-depth knowledge and establishing your channel as a go-to resource.

Cross-Promoting Videos within Playlists

Cross-promoting videos within playlists is a strategic way to maximize engagement and watch time on your YouTube channel. By guiding viewers through a curated journey of related content, you can keep them on your channel longer, increase the chances of them subscribing, and boost your overall channel performance. Here's an in-depth look at how to effectively cross-promote videos within playlists:

Benefits of Cross-Promoting Videos

1. Increased Watch Time:

Playlists encourage viewers to watch multiple videos in a row, significantly increasing overall watch time. This metric is crucial for YouTube's algorithm, which favors content that keeps viewers engaged longer.

2. Improved Viewer Retention:

By offering a seamless viewing experience with minimal interruptions, playlists help retain viewers. When one video ends and the next begins automatically, it reduces the likelihood of viewers clicking away.

3. Enhanced Discoverability:

Playlists improve the discoverability of your videos by grouping them together. Viewers interested in one video are likely to find related videos within the same playlist, increasing the visibility of your content.

4. Structured Content Delivery:

Playlists allow you to deliver content in a structured manner, making it easier for viewers to follow along. This is particularly useful for educational content, tutorials, or storytelling series.

Effective Cross-Promotion Strategies

1. Logical Sequencing:

Arrange videos in a logical sequence that makes sense for the viewer. For example, if you're creating a tutorial series, order the videos from beginner to advanced levels. Logical sequencing ensures a smooth viewing experience and encourages viewers to continue watching.

2. Clear Titles and Descriptions:

Use clear and descriptive titles for both your videos and playlists. Include keywords that accurately reflect the content to improve searchability.

Descriptions should outline what viewers can expect from the playlist and how the videos are connected.

3. Consistent Branding:

Maintain consistent branding across your playlist thumbnails, titles, and descriptions. Consistent visuals and messaging help viewers quickly identify your content and understand that the videos are part of a series.

4. Use of End Screens and Cards:

Incorporate end screens and cards in your videos to promote other videos within the same playlist. End screens can direct viewers to the next video in the series, while cards can be used throughout the video to suggest related content.

5. Verbal and Visual Cues:

Include verbal and visual cues within your videos to guide viewers to the playlist or the next video in the series. Phrases like "Check out the next video in this series" or on-screen text pointing to the playlist link can be effective.

6. Playlists in Descriptions:

Always include links to relevant playlists in your video descriptions.

This makes it easy for viewers to find and follow the series. Additionally, mention the playlist in your video to draw attention to it.

7. Highlight Playlists on Channel Page:

Feature key playlists prominently on your channel's homepage. Organize your channel layout to showcase these playlists, making them easily accessible to both new and returning viewers.

8. Collaborations and Guest Appearances:

Collaborate with other creators to create joint playlists that feature videos from both channels. This cross-promotion can introduce your content to a broader audience and drive more traffic to your playlists.

Monitoring and Optimization

1. Analyze Performance Metrics:

Use YouTube Analytics to monitor the performance of your playlists. Key metrics to track include watch time, average view duration, and viewer retention. Analyzing these metrics helps you understand how well your playlists are performing and where improvements can be made.

2. Adjust Based on Feedback:

Pay attention to viewer feedback in comments and social media. Use this feedback to refine your playlists and make adjustments that enhance viewer satisfaction and engagement.

3. Update Playlists Regularly:

Keep your playlists up to date by adding new relevant videos and removing outdated or underperforming content. Regular updates ensure that your playlists remain fresh and engaging for viewers.

4. Seasonal and Topical Playlists:

Create playlists around seasonal events, holidays, or trending topics. These timely playlists can attract viewers searching for specific content during particular times of the year, increasing your channel's relevance and reach.

Cross-promoting videos within playlists is an effective strategy to boost watch time, improve viewer retention, and enhance the overall performance of your YouTube channel. By logically sequencing videos, maintaining consistent branding, and utilizing tools like end screens and cards, you can guide viewers through a curated viewing experience that keeps them engaged and encourages them to explore more of your content.

Chapter 9
Analyzing YouTube Analytics

Key Metrics to Monitor

Monitoring key metrics on YouTube is essential for understanding the performance of your content and making data-driven decisions to improve your channel's growth and engagement. Here are the crucial metrics you should keep an eye on:

1. Watch Time

Definition:
The total amount of time viewers have spent watching your videos. This metric is a strong indicator of your content's overall appeal and engagement.

Importance:
Watch time is a significant factor in YouTube's algorithm for recommending videos. Higher watch time can lead to better visibility and more recommendations.

How to Monitor:
Check your YouTube Analytics to see the watch time for individual videos, playlists, and your channel as a whole. Aim to create content that keeps viewers watching for longer periods.

2. Average View Duration

Definition:
The average length of time viewers spend watching your videos.

Importance:
This metric helps you understand how engaging your content is. Longer average view durations indicate that viewers find your content interesting and worth watching till the end.

How to Monitor:
Analyze the average view duration for your videos in YouTube Analytics. Look for patterns in content that achieve higher durations and try to replicate those elements in future videos.

3. Audience Retention

Definition:
The percentage of your video that viewers watch, typically visualized as a graph showing where viewers drop off.

Importance:
High audience retention rates suggest that your content is engaging and maintains viewer interest. This is crucial for the algorithm and for converting casual viewers into subscribers.

How to Monitor:

Use the Audience Retention report in YouTube Analytics to see where viewers are dropping off. Identify any trends or common points of drop-off and adjust your content accordingly to keep viewers engaged.

4. Click-Through Rate (CTR)

Definition:
The percentage of people who click on your video after seeing the thumbnail and title.

Importance:
A high CTR indicates that your thumbnails and titles are compelling and effectively attracting viewers. It's the first step in getting viewers to watch your content.

How to Monitor:
Review the CTR data in YouTube Analytics. Test different thumbnails and titles to see what resonates best with your audience and improves your CTR.

5. Impressions

Definition:
The number of times your video thumbnails were shown to viewers on YouTube.

Importance:

Impressions measure the reach of your videos. More impressions can lead to higher views, provided your CTR is strong.

How to Monitor:
Track the number of impressions in YouTube Analytics. Aim to increase impressions by optimizing your video's SEO, promoting your videos, and encouraging shares.

6. Engagement Metrics (Likes, Comments, Shares)

Definition:
Metrics that indicate viewer interaction with your content, including likes, comments, and shares.

Importance:
Engagement metrics reflect how much your audience interacts with your content. High engagement can boost your video's ranking and lead to more organic reach.

How to Monitor:
Monitor the number of likes, comments, and shares for each video in YouTube Analytics. Encourage engagement by asking viewers to like, comment, and share.

7. Subscriber Growth

Definition:
The number of new subscribers gained over a specific period.

Importance:
Subscriber growth indicates your channel's ability to attract and retain viewers. Subscribers are more likely to watch your new videos and engage with your content.

How to Monitor:
Check your subscriber count and growth trends in YouTube Analytics. Analyze what types of content or specific videos lead to spikes in subscriber numbers.

8. Traffic Sources

Definition:
The origins of your video views, such as YouTube search, suggested videos, external sources, and direct traffic.

Importance:

Understanding where your viewers come from helps you focus your promotional efforts and optimize your content for those sources.

How to Monitor:
Review the Traffic Sources report in YouTube Analytics. Identify the most effective sources and consider investing more effort in those areas.

9. Demographics

Definition:
Information about the age, gender, location, and device used by your viewers.

Importance:
Knowing your audience demographics helps tailor your content to better suit your viewers' preferences and optimize your marketing strategies.

How to Monitor:
Analyze the Demographics report in YouTube Analytics to understand who your viewers are. Use this information to create targeted content and marketing campaigns.

10. Revenue Metrics (for Monetized Channels)

Definition:
Metrics related to the earnings from your YouTube channel, including ad revenue, channel memberships, and Super Chats.

Importance:
For monetized channels, tracking revenue metrics is crucial for understanding the financial performance and identifying opportunities to increase earnings.

How to Monitor:
Review the Revenue report in YouTube Analytics to see how much you're earning from ads and other monetization methods. Look for trends and explore new ways to increase your channel's revenue.

Regularly monitoring these key metrics provides valuable insights into your channel's performance and viewer behavior. By analyzing these data points, you can make informed decisions to optimize your content strategy, enhance viewer engagement, and drive sustained growth for your YouTube channel. Use these insights to continually refine your approach, ensuring that your content remains relevant, engaging, and successful.

Moreover, staying attuned to these metrics allows you to identify trends and patterns that can inform future content creation. For instance, if you notice a particular type of video consistently performs well, you can focus on producing more of that content. Conversely, if certain videos have lower engagement, you can analyze what might be causing viewers to lose interest and make necessary adjustments.

Understanding Traffic Sources

Understanding traffic sources is crucial for optimizing your YouTube channel's growth and engagement. Traffic sources reveal where your viewers are coming from, enabling you to tailor your content and promotional strategies to maximize reach and retention. Here's an in-depth look at the different types of traffic sources and how to leverage them effectively:

Types of Traffic Sources

1. YouTube Search:

- **Definition:** Views generated from users searching for keywords on YouTube.
- **Importance:** Indicates how well your videos are optimized for search queries. A high volume of search traffic suggests effective use of SEO (Search Engine Optimization).
- **Optimization Tips**: Use relevant keywords in your titles, descriptions, and tags. Conduct keyword research to find popular search terms in your niche. Create content that addresses common questions or topics your target audience is searching for.

2. Suggested Videos:

- **Definition:** Views from videos recommended by YouTube's algorithm.

- **Importance:** Suggested videos can drive significant traffic by capturing the attention of viewers who are already watching similar content.
- **Optimization Tips:** Create engaging thumbnails and compelling titles. Maintain high audience retention and engagement rates to increase the likelihood of being suggested. Cross-promote your own videos within your content to keep viewers on your channel.

3. External Sources:

- **Definition:** Views coming from outside of YouTube, such as social media platforms, websites, and blogs.
- **Importance:** Expands your reach beyond YouTube's ecosystem and taps into new audiences.
- **Optimization Tips:** Promote your videos on social media platforms like Facebook, Twitter, Instagram, and LinkedIn. Embed videos in blog posts and on your website. Collaborate with influencers and other content creators to share your videos with their audiences.

4. Browse Features:

- **Definition:** Views from YouTube's homepage, subscriptions feed, and other browsing features.

- **Importance:** Indicates how often your content is featured on YouTube's main interface, which can significantly boost visibility.
- **Optimization Tips:** Post videos at times when your subscribers are most active. Engage with your audience through community posts and polls to increase visibility in the subscriptions feed. Consistently upload high-quality content to maintain a strong presence on the homepage.

5. Channel Pages:

- **Definition:** Views originating from your channel page.
- **Importance:** Reflects the effectiveness of your channel layout and the appeal of your content to existing and potential subscribers.
- **Optimization Tips:** Organize your channel page with playlists and featured sections. Create a compelling channel trailer that highlights your best content. Use consistent branding across your channel to create a professional and cohesive look.

6. Direct or Unknown:

- **Definition:** Views from unknown or direct sources, such as links clicked directly from email or offline promotions.

- **Importance:** Can be difficult to track but still valuable for understanding overall traffic.
- **Optimization Tips:** Use custom URLs and tracking codes to better understand direct traffic. Encourage email subscribers to watch your videos through newsletters and updates.

7. Notifications:

- **Definition:** Views generated from notifications sent to subscribers when you upload a new video or go live.
- **Importance:** Indicates how effectively you are engaging with your subscriber base.
- **Optimization Tips:** Encourage viewers to subscribe and turn on notifications. Regularly post content to maintain subscriber interest and engagement.

Leveraging Traffic Sources for Growth

1. Analyzing Traffic Sources:

Use YouTube Analytics to track the performance of different traffic sources. Identify which sources are driving the most views and engagement, and focus your efforts on optimizing those channels.

2. Tailoring Content for Different Sources:

Create content that is optimized for the strengths of each traffic source.

For example, SEO-friendly videos for YouTube search, shareable content for social media, and visually appealing thumbnails for suggested videos.

3. Promoting Across Platforms:

Cross-promote your videos on various platforms to diversify your traffic sources. Use social media, email marketing, and collaborations to reach wider audiences.

4. Engaging with Your Audience:

Engage with your audience on the platforms that drive the most traffic. Respond to comments, participate in discussions, and create content based on viewer feedback and preferences.

5. Testing and Iterating:

Continuously test different strategies to see what works best for each traffic source. Experiment with different titles, thumbnails, descriptions, and posting times to optimize your reach and engagement.

Understanding and optimizing your traffic sources is vital for driving sustained growth and engagement on your YouTube channel.

Utilizing Analytics to Improve Content

Leveraging YouTube Analytics is essential for understanding how your content is performing and identifying areas for improvement. By thoroughly analyzing the data provided, you can make informed decisions to enhance your content strategy, boost viewer engagement, and grow your channel. Here's how to effectively use YouTube Analytics to improve your content:

Strategies for Utilizing Analytics

1. Identify Top-Performing Content:

Use analytics to determine which videos have the highest watch time, engagement, and CTR. Analyze the common elements in these videos and replicate their successful features in your future content.

2. Optimize Video Length and Structure:

Review audience retention data to find the optimal length for your videos. Ensure that your content is structured in a way that maintains viewer interest from start to finish. Avoid lengthy introductions and get to the main points quickly to retain viewers.

3. Improve SEO:

Analyze search traffic sources to understand what keywords and search terms lead viewers to your videos. Optimize your titles, descriptions, and tags with these keywords to improve discoverability. Use tools like Google Trends and YouTube's search suggestions to find relevant keywords.

4. Enhance Thumbnails and Titles:

Experiment with different thumbnail designs and title formats to see what generates the highest CTR. Thumbnails should be visually appealing and accurately represent the content of the video. Titles should be compelling and include relevant keywords.

5. Tailor Content to Audience Preferences:

Use demographic data to create content that resonates with your audience's preferences. For example, if your audience is predominantly younger, consider trends and topics that appeal to that age group. If you have a global audience, consider creating content with universal appeal or adding subtitles in different languages.

6. Promote Engagement:

Encourage viewers to like, comment, and share your videos.

Engage with your audience in the comments section and on social media to build a community around your content. Higher engagement can lead to better performance in YouTube's algorithm.

7. Schedule Consistent Uploads:

Use analytics to determine the best times and days to upload your videos based on when your audience is most active. Consistency in your upload schedule can improve viewer retention and engagement.

8. Monitor and Adapt:

Regularly review your analytics to stay informed about your channel's performance. Be flexible and willing to adapt your content strategy based on the data. Continuously test new ideas and approaches to see what works best for your audience.

Utilizing YouTube Analytics effectively can transform your content strategy and drive significant growth for your channel. By understanding key metrics like watch time, audience retention, CTR, demographics, and traffic sources, you can make data-driven decisions that enhance your content and engagement. Regularly monitoring and adapting based on analytics will ensure your content remains relevant, engaging, and successful.

Chapter 10
Utilizing YouTube's Advanced Features

YouTube Stories and Community Posts

YouTube Stories and Community Posts are powerful tools that enable creators to engage with their audience in dynamic and interactive ways. Both features offer unique benefits and can significantly enhance your channel's growth and viewer engagement. Here's a detailed look at how to effectively utilize YouTube Stories and Community Posts:

YouTube Stories

Definition:

YouTube Stories are short, mobile-only videos that expire after seven days. This feature is available to channels with over 10,000 subscribers.

Benefits:

- Engages your audience with short, frequent updates.
- Provides a casual, behind-the-scenes look at your channel.

How to Use YouTube Stories Effectively:

Behind the Scenes Content:

Share behind-the-scenes footage of your video production process. This gives viewers a glimpse into your daily routine and helps build a personal connection.

Quick Updates:

Use Stories to provide quick updates about upcoming videos, events, or channel milestones. This keeps your audience informed and excited about what's next.

Promote New Content:

Tease new videos or series with short clips or previews. Encourage viewers to check out the full content by adding a direct link to your latest video.

Engage with Your Audience:

Use interactive features like polls and questions to engage with your audience. Ask for their opinions, conduct surveys, or simply start a conversation to foster community interaction.

Highlight Fan Contributions:

Showcase fan art, comments, or responses to your content. This not only recognizes your audience's contributions but also encourages more engagement.

Behind-the-Scenes Insights:

Provide exclusive insights or tips related to your content niche. Share quick tutorials, fun facts, or personal anecdotes to add value to your Stories.

Real-Time Interaction:

Use Stories during live events or while attending conferences to share real-time updates. This helps create a sense of immediacy and involvement for your viewers.

YouTube Community Posts

Definition:

Community Posts are text, image, GIF, or poll updates shared in the Community tab of your YouTube channel. This feature is available to channels with over 500 subscribers.

Benefits:

- Keeps your audience engaged between video uploads.
- Allows for direct interaction and feedback.
- Helps maintain a consistent presence on your channel.

How to Use YouTube Community Posts Effectively:

Announcements and Updates:

Share important channel updates, such as new video releases, schedule changes, or milestones. Keep your audience informed about what's happening on your channel.

Promote Upcoming Content:

Tease upcoming videos or series with images, GIFs, or brief descriptions. Build anticipation and provide a glimpse of what viewers can expect.

Engage with Polls:

Create polls to gather feedback, understand viewer preferences, or make decisions about future content. Polls are an excellent way to involve your audience in your creative process.

Share Exclusive Content:

Post exclusive behind-the-scenes photos, previews, or bloopers that don't make it into your videos. This adds a personal touch and gives your audience something special.

Celebrate Milestones:

Acknowledge and celebrate subscriber milestones, anniversaries, or significant achievements. Thank your viewers for their support and make them feel part of your journey.

Conduct Q&A Sessions:

Use Community Posts to host Q&A sessions. Encourage viewers to ask questions, and then respond directly in the comments or through dedicated Q&A videos.

Highlight Viewer Contributions:

Showcase fan art, favorite comments, or video responses from your audience. This fosters a sense of community and appreciation among your viewers.

Share Relevant Content:

Post links to relevant articles, videos, or external content that your audience might find interesting or valuable.

Integrating Stories and Community Posts into Your Strategy

1. Maintain Regular Engagement:

Use Stories for frequent, informal updates and Community Posts for more substantial interactions. This combination keeps your audience engaged between video uploads and fosters a consistent connection.

2. Encourage Viewer Interaction:

Prompt your audience to interact with your Stories and Posts. Ask questions, seek feedback, and respond to comments to build a lively and engaged community.

3. Cross-Promote Content:

Promote your Stories in your Community Posts and vice versa. Encourage viewers to check out your Stories for more casual, behind-the-scenes content and use Community Posts for in-depth updates and discussions.

4. Analyze Performance:

Monitor the performance of your Stories and Community Posts through YouTube Analytics.

YouTube Stories and Community Posts are valuable tools for maintaining an active and engaged audience. By sharing behind-the-scenes content, providing updates, and encouraging interaction, you can create a dynamic and interactive experience for your viewers. Utilize these features to complement your video content, foster a sense of community, and drive long-term growth for your YouTube channel. Regularly monitor their performance and adapt your strategy to ensure you are effectively engaging with your audience and meeting their interests and expectations.

Furthermore, integrating these tools can help you maintain visibility and engagement even during periods when you are not uploading new videos. This consistent interaction keeps your channel relevant and top-of-mind for your audience. By experimenting with different types of posts and stories, you can discover what content resonates best with your viewers, allowing you to refine your approach and deliver value consistently.

Additionally, leveraging Stories and Community Posts can provide insights into your audience's preferences and behaviors. Analyzing the engagement and feedback from these posts can guide your future content creation, ensuring it aligns with what your audience finds most engaging and entertaining.

Premiere and Live Streaming

YouTube Premiere and Live Streaming are powerful tools for enhancing viewer engagement and creating a sense of community around your content. Each offers unique benefits and can significantly boost your channel's growth and viewer interaction. Here's an in-depth look at how to effectively utilize YouTube Premiere and Live Streaming:

YouTube Premiere

Definition:

YouTube Premiere allows creators to upload and schedule a video to play at a specific time as a live event, providing a shared viewing experience for the audience.

Benefits:

- Builds anticipation and excitement for new content.
- Creates a live viewing experience with real-time interaction.
- Enhances viewer engagement through live chat.
- Encourages community building and viewer loyalty.
- Provides an opportunity for immediate feedback and discussion.

How to Use YouTube Premiere Effectively:

Build Anticipation:

Promote your Premiere in advance across your social media platforms and YouTube Community Posts. Create teasers or countdowns to build excitement.

Engage with Live Chat:

Participate in the live chat during the Premiere to interact with your audience. Answer questions, respond to comments, and engage in conversations to foster a sense of community.

Schedule Strategically:

Choose a time for your Premiere when your audience is most active. Use YouTube Analytics to determine the optimal time to maximize viewership.

Create a Hype:

Use compelling thumbnails and titles to attract viewers. Consider adding an intriguing description that encourages viewers to join the Premiere.

Post-Premiere Engagement:

After the Premiere, keep the conversation going in the comments section.

Thank viewers for joining and encourage them to share their thoughts and feedback.

YouTube Live Streaming

Definition:

Live Streaming on YouTube allows creators to broadcast in real-time, providing an immediate and interactive experience for viewers.

Benefits:

- Offers real-time interaction with your audience.
- Increases viewer engagement and builds a stronger community.
- Provides opportunities for spontaneous and authentic content.

How to Use YouTube Live Streaming Effectively:

Plan Your Stream:

Plan your live stream content in advance. Have a clear agenda, whether it's a Q&A session, a live tutorial, a gaming session, or an event coverage.

Promote Ahead of Time:

Announce your live stream in advance to give your audience time to prepare. Use social media, Community Posts.

Engage Actively:

Interact with your viewers during the live stream. Respond to comments, answer questions, and acknowledge new viewers. Active engagement keeps viewers interested and enhances the live experience.

Use Quality Equipment:

Ensure you have a good quality camera and microphone to provide a clear and professional streaming experience. Stable internet connection is crucial for a smooth stream.

Incorporate Interactive Elements:

Use features like live polls, super chats, and interactive overlays to keep the audience engaged. Encourage viewers to participate and make them feel involved in the stream.

Monitor Analytics:

After your live stream, review the analytics to understand viewer behavior, engagement, and retention. Use these insights to improve future live streams.

Integrating Premiere and Live Streaming into Your Strategy

1. Enhance Viewer Engagement:

Both Premiere and Live Streaming create a sense of immediacy and exclusivity, encouraging viewers to join in real-time and engage more actively with your content.

2. Foster Community Interaction:

Use these tools to build a strong sense of community. Regularly scheduled Premieres and live streams can become events that your audience looks forward to, fostering a loyal viewer base.

3. Diversify Content:

Incorporate a mix of pre-recorded videos, Premieres, and live streams to diversify your content offering. This keeps your channel dynamic and caters to different viewer preferences.

4. Maximize Exposure:

Promote your Premieres and live streams across all your social media platforms and YouTube features. The more visibility and anticipation you build, the higher the engagement and viewer turnout.

5. Collect Real-Time Feedback:

Use the interactive nature of live streams and Premieres to collect real-time feedback from your audience. This immediate feedback can guide your content strategy and improve viewer satisfaction.

YouTube Premiere and Live Streaming are invaluable tools for increasing engagement, building community, and driving channel growth. By creating live, interactive experiences, you can connect with your audience on a deeper level and foster a loyal viewer base. Utilize these features strategically, promoting them in advance and engaging actively during the events to maximize their impact. Regularly integrating Premieres and live streams into your content strategy will ensure a dynamic, engaging, and successful YouTube channel.

Furthermore, these features allow you to collect real-time feedback and adapt your content to meet viewer preferences more effectively. The immediate interaction during live events helps build trust and authenticity, making your audience feel valued and heard. As you continue to experiment and refine your use of Premieres and live streams, you'll be able to create more compelling and interactive content that resonates with your viewers, ultimately leading to sustained growth and long-term success for your channel.

Cards and End Screens

Definition:

Cards and End Screens are interactive elements you can add to your YouTube videos to promote other content, encourage viewer actions, and enhance the overall viewing experience.

Cards

Cards are small, transparent notifications that appear in the upper-right corner of a video. They can be used to link to other videos, playlists, channels, websites, polls, and fundraising sites.

Benefits:

- Directs viewers to additional content, keeping them engaged with your channel.
- Can be timed to appear at the most relevant moments in your video.
- Enhances viewer interaction and retention by providing more viewing options.

How to Use Cards Effectively:

Promote Related Videos:

Use cards to link to related videos or playlists. This can help maintain viewer interest and keep them on your channel longer.

Encourage Channel Subscriptions:

Add cards that link to your channel page with a call-to-action to subscribe. This can be particularly effective towards the end of the video when viewers have engaged with your content.

Poll Your Audience:

Use cards to create polls and gather viewer feedback. This not only increases interaction but also provides valuable insights into your audience's preferences and opinions.

Highlight Collaborations:

If you collaborate with other creators, use cards to link to their channels or videos. This can introduce your audience to new content and foster goodwill between channels.

Promote Merchandise and Fundraising:

Link to your merchandise store or fundraising campaigns using cards. This can be an effective way to monetize your channel and support causes you care about.

End Screens

End Screens are interactive elements that appear in the last 5-20 seconds of a video.

Benefits:

- Provides a structured way to keep viewers engaged after the video ends.
- Increases watch time by directing viewers to additional content.
- Enhances the likelihood of viewers subscribing or taking other actions.

How to Use End Screens Effectively:

Promote Next Video:

Suggest a next video for viewers to watch. This could be a related video or the next episode in a series. Clear calls-to-action encourage viewers to continue watching.

Encourage Subscriptions:

Add a subscription button to your end screen. Make it visually appealing and include a friendly reminder to subscribe if viewers enjoyed the content.

Highlight Playlists:

Link to playlists that organize your content by theme or series. This helps viewers find more of what they like and can significantly boost watch time.

Feature Collaborators:

Promote channels of collaborators or other creators. This not only supports fellow YouTubers but can also introduce your audience to new content they might enjoy.

Direct to External Links:

Use end screens to direct viewers to your website, social media profiles, or other external links. This can drive traffic to your other platforms and expand your online presence.

Integrating Cards and End Screens into Your Strategy

1. Plan Strategically:

Integrate cards and end screens into your video planning process. Determine the most logical points in your video to insert cards and design end screens that guide viewers seamlessly to their next action.

2. Analyze Performance:

Use YouTube Analytics to track the performance of your cards and end screens. Pay attention to click-through rates and viewer behavior to refine your strategy and maximize effectiveness.

3. Keep it Relevant:

Ensure that the content you promote with cards and end screens is relevant to the current video. Irrelevant promotions can disrupt the viewer experience and decrease engagement.

4. Test and Optimize:

Experiment with different types of cards and end screens to see what resonates best with your audience. Test various placements, calls-to-action, and designs to optimize performance.

5. Maintain Visual Consistency:

Design end screens that match your channel's branding. Consistent visuals help reinforce your brand identity and provide a cohesive viewing experience.

Cards and End Screens are essential tools for enhancing viewer engagement, increasing watch time, and promoting additional content on your YouTube channel. By strategically implementing these interactive elements, you can guide viewers to take desired actions, whether it's watching another video, subscribing to your channel, or visiting an external link. Regularly analyzing their performance and optimizing their use will help you maximize their impact, ultimately contributing to the sustained growth and success of your YouTube channel.

Chapter 11
Monetization Strategies

Meeting YouTube's Monetization Requirements

Meeting YouTube's monetization requirements involves several key steps and ongoing commitments to ensure your channel can generate revenue through ads, memberships, and other monetization features. Here's a comprehensive guide to help you navigate this process:

1. Understanding the Basics

To be eligible for YouTube's Partner Program (YPP), which allows you to monetize your videos, your channel must meet the following criteria:

- 1,000 subscribers: This is the minimum number of subscribers your channel must have.
- 4,000 watch hours: Your content must have accumulated at least 4,000 valid public watch hours within the last 12 months.
- AdSense Account: You need to have an AdSense account linked to your YouTube channel for receiving payments.

2. Creating Quality Content
Consistency and quality are crucial for growing your subscriber base and watch hours.

Focus on creating engaging, informative, or entertaining content that resonates with your target audience. Regular uploads, preferably on a fixed schedule, can help maintain viewer interest and encourage repeat visits.

3. Engaging with Your Audience

Building a loyal community is essential. Respond to comments, engage in conversations, and encourage viewers to like, share, and subscribe. Active engagement signals to YouTube that your channel has an active and invested audience, which can positively impact your channel's growth.

4. Optimizing Video SEO

Utilize SEO strategies to improve your video's visibility. This includes:

- Titles: Craft compelling and keyword-rich titles.
- Descriptions: Write detailed descriptions with relevant keywords and timestamps.
- Tags: Use appropriate tags to categorize your content.
- Thumbnails: Create eye-catching thumbnails that accurately represent your content.

5. Maintaining Compliance

Ensure your content complies with YouTube's policies, including Community Guidelines, Terms of Service, and AdSense policies.

Avoid content that promotes violence, hate speech, or any form of misleading information. Staying compliant not only helps in monetization but also protects your channel from potential strikes and bans.

6. Enabling Monetization Features

Once you meet the eligibility requirements, you can apply for the YouTube Partner Program:

- Application Process: Apply through the YouTube Studio by following the monetization prompts.
- Review: YouTube will review your channel to ensure it meets all guidelines.
- Approval: If approved, you can start monetizing your videos by enabling ads and other revenue streams.

7. Exploring Additional Monetization Options

Beyond ads, YouTube offers several other monetization features:

- Channel Memberships: Offer exclusive perks to subscribers for a monthly fee.
- Super Chat and Super Stickers: Enable viewers to pay for highlighted messages during live streams.
- Merchandise Shelf: Showcase and sell your branded merchandise directly on your channel.

8. Analyzing Performance

Regularly review your YouTube Analytics to understand what content performs best and where your audience is coming from. Use these insights to refine your content strategy and improve your channel's performance over time.

9. Staying Updated

YouTube frequently updates its policies and features. Stay informed about any changes by regularly checking YouTube's Creator Blog and Help Center. Adapting to these changes promptly ensures your channel remains in good standing and continues to meet monetization requirements.

Meeting YouTube's monetization requirements is a blend of strategic planning, consistent content creation, active audience engagement, and compliance with platform policies. By following these guidelines, you can effectively navigate the monetization process and set your channel up for long-term success and revenue generation.

Moreover, diversifying your content and revenue streams can further enhance your channel's sustainability and profitability. Experiment with different video formats, such as tutorials, vlogs, and live streams, to keep your content fresh and appealing.

AdSense and Partner Programs: A Comprehensive Guide to YouTube Monetization

Monetizing your YouTube channel through AdSense and the YouTube Partner Program (YPP) involves several steps, requirements, and ongoing responsibilities. This guide provides an in-depth look at how these systems work and how you can optimize your channel for maximum revenue.

Understanding AdSense

Google AdSense is a program that allows creators to earn money by displaying ads on their websites, blogs, or YouTube videos. Here's how it works for YouTube:

Creating an AdSense Account:

- **Sign Up:** Visit the AdSense website and sign up for an account. If you already have an AdSense account for another website, you can link it to your YouTube channel.
- **Linking to YouTube:** In the YouTube Studio, go to the monetization section and link your AdSense account. This will enable YouTube to pay you through AdSense.

Ad Formats:

- **Display Ads:** These appear beside your video.

- **Overlay Ads:** Semi-transparent ads that appear at the bottom of your video.
- **Skippable Video Ads:** Viewers can skip these ads after 5 seconds.
- **Non-Skippable Video Ads:** Viewers must watch the entire ad before your video.
- **Bumper Ads:** Short, non-skippable ads up to 6 seconds.
- **Sponsored Cards:** These show content relevant to your video, like products featured in the video.

Revenue Share:

YouTube takes a 45% cut of ad revenue, and creators receive the remaining 55%.

Joining the YouTube Partner Program (YPP)

The YPP provides creators with access to more robust monetization features beyond just ads. Here's how to join and what it entails:

Eligibility Requirements:

- **1,000 Subscribers:** Your channel must have at least 1,000 subscribers.
- **4,000 Watch Hours:** You need at least 4,000 valid public watch hours within the past 12 months.
- **Adherence to Policies:** Your content must comply with YouTube's Community Guidelines, Terms of Service, and AdSense policies.

- **Two-Step Verification:** Enable two-step verification on your Google account for added security.

Application Process:

- **Apply:** In the YouTube Studio, navigate to the Monetization tab and click "Apply Now".
- **Review:** YouTube will review your channel to ensure it meets all requirements. This process can take a few weeks.
- **Approval:** If approved, you can enable monetization on your videos and access additional features.

Monetization Features:

- **Ads:** Enable different types of ads on your videos.
- **Channel Memberships:** Offer exclusive perks to subscribers for a monthly fee.
- **Super Chat and Super Stickers:** Viewers can pay to have their messages highlighted during live chats.
- **Merchandise Shelf:** Display and sell your branded merchandise directly on your channel.
- **YouTube Premium Revenue:** Earn a share of the subscription fee when YouTube Premium members watch your content.

Optimizing Your Revenue

Content Strategy:

- **High-Engagement Content:** Create content that encourages viewers to watch longer and engage more.
- **Regular Uploads:** Maintain a consistent upload schedule to keep viewers coming back.

SEO and Promotion:

- **Keywords:** Use relevant keywords in your titles, descriptions, and tags.
- **Thumbnails:** Design eye-catching thumbnails to increase click-through rates.
- **Social Media:** Promote your videos across social media platforms to reach a wider audience.

Compliance and Quality:

- **Follow Guidelines:** Adhere to all of YouTube's policies to avoid penalties or demonetization.
- **High-Quality Content:** Invest in good equipment and editing to produce high-quality videos that attract more viewers.

Good production values not only improve the overall viewing experience but also increase viewer engagement and retention.

Managing Your AdSense Account

Payment Threshold:

You need to earn at least $100 before AdSense will pay you. Payments are made monthly, provided you meet the threshold.

Payment Methods:

Set up your preferred payment method in AdSense, such as direct deposit or checks.

Taxes:

Ensure you provide the necessary tax information to AdSense to comply with your country's tax laws.

Conclusion

AdSense and the YouTube Partner Program offer multiple avenues for monetizing your content, but success requires strategic planning, consistent effort, and adherence to guidelines. By understanding and leveraging these tools effectively, you can build a sustainable income stream from your YouTube channel, allowing you to focus on creating engaging and high-quality content for your audience.

Exploring Alternative Revenue Streams for YouTube Creators

In addition to ad revenue from AdSense and the YouTube Partner Program (YPP), there are numerous alternative revenue streams that YouTube creators can leverage to diversify their income and increase financial stability. Here's an in-depth look at these alternatives:

1. Channel Memberships

Channel Memberships allow your viewers to support you directly on YouTube by paying a monthly fee in exchange for exclusive perks.

- **Exclusive Content:** Offer members-only videos, live streams, and posts.
- **Badges and Emojis:** Provide custom badges and emojis that members can use in comments and live chats.
- **Member Shoutouts:** Acknowledge your members in your videos or live streams to foster a sense of community.

2. Merchandise Sales

Selling branded merchandise is a popular way for creators to generate additional income.

- **Merchandise Shelf:** Use YouTube's Merchandise Shelf to display your products directly under your videos.

- **E-commerce Platforms:** Set up a store on platforms like Teespring, Spreadshirt, or Shopify.
- **Product Ideas:** T-shirts, hoodies, mugs, stickers, and other branded items that resonate with your audience.

3. Affiliate Marketing

Affiliate marketing involves promoting products or services and earning a commission on any sales made through your referral links.

- **Partnerships:** Collaborate with brands relevant to your niche.
- **Affiliate Networks:** Join networks like Amazon Associates, ShareASale, or Commission Junction to find products to promote.
- **Integration:** Include affiliate links in your video descriptions, and create content that naturally incorporates the products.

4. Sponsored Content

Brands often seek out YouTubers to create sponsored content promoting their products or services.

- **Direct Sponsorships:** Negotiate deals directly with brands for sponsored videos or shoutouts.
- **Influencer Platforms:** Use platforms like FameBit, Grapevine, or Channel Pages to connect with brands looking for influencers.

- **Transparency:** Always disclose sponsored content to maintain transparency and trust with your audience.

5. Crowdfunding and Donations

Platforms like Patreon and PayPal allow your viewers to support your channel through one-time donations or recurring contributions.

- **Patreon:** Offer tiered membership levels with exclusive rewards for patrons.
- **PayPal Donations:** Set up a PayPal link for one-time donations.
- **YouTube Features:** Use YouTube's Super Chat and Super Stickers during live streams to allow viewers to pay for highlighted messages.

6. Online Courses and Workshops

If you have expertise in a particular area, consider creating and selling online courses or conducting workshops.

- **Platforms:** Use platforms like Udemy, Teachable, or Skillshare to host your courses.
- **Content:** Develop comprehensive tutorials, masterclasses, or training sessions that provide value to your audience.
- **Promotion:** Promote your courses through your YouTube channel and other social media platforms.

7. Digital Products

Selling digital products such as e-books, presets, templates, or printables can be a lucrative revenue stream.

- **E-books:** Write an e-book related to your niche and sell it on Amazon Kindle or your own website.
- **Digital Downloads:** Offer photography presets, video templates, or printable resources.
- **Content Bundles:** Create bundles of your best content or resources for a one-time purchase.

8. Licensing Your Content

If your videos contain high-quality, unique content, you can license them to other media outlets.

- **Stock Footage:** Sell your video clips as stock footage on sites like Shutterstock, Pond5, or Adobe Stock.
- **Media Outlets:** License your content to news organizations, production companies, or other creators.

9. Public Speaking and Appearances

As your channel grows, you may receive opportunities for public speaking or appearances.

- **Speaking Engagements:** Speak at conferences, workshops, or industry events.
- **Panel Discussions:** Participate in panel discussions related to your niche.
- **Guest Appearances:** Make guest appearances on podcasts, webinars, or other YouTube channels.

Exploring alternative revenue streams is essential for building a resilient and diversified income as a YouTube creator. By diversifying your revenue sources, such as through channel memberships, merchandise sales, and crowdfunding platforms like Patreon or Kickstarter, you can mitigate the risks associated with relying solely on ad revenue. Channel memberships offer subscribers exclusive perks in exchange for a monthly fee, fostering a sense of community and providing consistent revenue.

Merchandise sales, facilitated through YouTube's merchandise shelf, allow you to sell branded products directly to your audience, leveraging your channel's brand identity. Crowdfunding platforms enable fans to support your content directly, offering a more intimate connection with your most dedicated followers.

This diversification not only enhances your financial stability but also allows you to focus more on creating the content you love.

Chapter 12
Building a Strong Brand on YouTube
Creating a Cohesive Channel Identity

Creating a cohesive channel identity is crucial for building a strong and recognizable brand on YouTube. Here's a detailed guide to help you establish and maintain a consistent identity for your channel:

1. Define Your Niche and Target Audience

- **Identify Your Niche:** Choose a specific area of focus for your channel, such as personal finance, investing, lifestyle, or tech reviews. This helps attract a dedicated audience.
- **Understand Your Audience:** Research your target audience's demographics, interests, and pain points. Tailor your content to meet their needs and preferences.

2. Develop a Unique Value Proposition

- **What Makes You Unique:** Clearly articulate what sets your channel apart from others in the same niche. This could be your unique perspective, expertise, or style of presentation.
- **Value to Viewers:** Define the specific benefits viewers will gain from watching your videos, such as actionable advice, entertainment, or education.

3. Create Consistent Visual Branding

- **Logo and Channel Art:** Design a memorable logo and channel banner that reflects your channel's identity. Use consistent colors, fonts, and imagery across all visual elements.
- **Thumbnails:** Develop a recognizable thumbnail style. Use consistent fonts, colors, and layouts to make your videos instantly identifiable.

4. Develop a Content Strategy

- **Content Pillars:** Identify the main themes or topics your channel will cover. This helps maintain a clear focus and ensures your content is aligned with your niche.
- **Upload Schedule:** Establish a regular posting schedule to keep your audience engaged and coming back for more. Consistency helps build trust and anticipation.

5. Craft a Signature Style

- **Tone and Voice:** Determine the tone and voice of your channel. Whether it's professional, casual, humorous, or inspirational, ensure it aligns with your brand and resonates with your audience.
- **Presentation Style:** Decide on your on-camera presence, including your speaking style, body language, and interaction with the audience.

6. Utilize Branding Elements in Videos

- **Intro and Outro:** Create a consistent intro and outro for your videos. This can include a branded animation, tagline, or call-to-action.
- **Watermarks and Overlays:** Use watermarks, lower thirds, and other on-screen graphics that reinforce your brand identity.

7. Engage with Your Audience

- **Community Building:** Foster a sense of community by engaging with your audience through comments, social media, and live streams. Show appreciation for their support and feedback.
- **Viewer Interaction:** Encourage viewers to like, comment, and subscribe. Respond to comments and create content based on viewer suggestions and questions.

8. Optimize Your Channel Page

- **About Section:** Write a compelling channel description that clearly explains who you are, what your channel is about, and what viewers can expect.
- **Playlists:** Organize your videos into playlists based on themes or topics. This helps viewers find relevant content and increases watch time.

9. Collaborate and Network

- **Collaborations:** Partner with other YouTubers or influencers in your niche. This can help you reach a wider audience and add credibility to your channel.
- **Networking:** Attend industry events, participate in online forums, and join social media groups to connect with others in your field.

10. Monitor and Adjust

- **Analytics:** Regularly review your channel analytics to understand what's working and what's not. Use insights to refine your content strategy and improve viewer engagement.
- **Feedback:** Pay attention to viewer feedback and adapt your content and branding accordingly. Stay flexible and open to change.

By following these steps, you can create a cohesive and compelling channel identity that attracts and retains viewers, builds loyalty, and sets you apart in the crowded YouTube landscape. By developing a strong channel identity, you also pave the way for potential monetization opportunities and partnerships. Brands are more likely to collaborate with channels that have a clear, consistent identity and a loyal following.

Designing Effective Channel Art and Logos

Designing effective channel art and logos is a fundamental aspect of establishing a cohesive and visually appealing brand on YouTube. Here's a comprehensive guide to help you create standout visual elements for your channel:

1. Understand the Importance of Channel Art and Logos

- **First Impressions:** Channel art and logos are often the first things viewers notice. They set the tone for your brand and can entice viewers to explore your content.
- **Brand Recognition:** Consistent and memorable visual branding helps viewers instantly recognize your channel across various platforms and media.

2. Define Your Visual Identity

- **Brand Colors:** Choose a color palette that reflects your brand's personality and appeals to your target audience. Stick to a few key colors to maintain consistency.
- **Typography:** Select fonts that complement your brand style. Use one or two fonts consistently across all your branding materials.
- **Imagery and Style:** Decide on the types of images and graphic styles that align with your brand.

3. Designing Your Logo

- **Simplicity:** A good logo is simple and easily recognizable. Avoid clutter and keep the design clean.
- **Scalability:** Ensure your logo looks good at all sizes, from small social media icons to larger formats like channel banners.
- **Relevance:** Your logo should represent your channel's content and values. It should give viewers a sense of what your channel is about.
- **Uniqueness:** Stand out from the crowd with a unique logo. Avoid generic designs and strive for something that reflects your distinct brand identity.

4. Creating Channel Art

- **Dimensions and Layout:** YouTube channel art (or banners) should be 2560 x 1440 pixels. Ensure important elements like text and logos are within the safe area (1546 x 423 pixels) to be visible on all devices.
- **Incorporate Key Information:** Include your channel name, tagline, and a brief description of your content. Consider adding your upload schedule to let viewers know when to expect new videos.
- **Visual Hierarchy:** Use size, color, and positioning to guide the viewer's eye to the most important elements of your channel art.

- **Brand Consistency:** Ensure your channel art aligns with your overall brand aesthetics. Use the same colors, fonts, and styles as in your logo and thumbnails.

5. Tools and Resources for Design

- **Graphic Design Software:** Use tools like Adobe Photoshop, Illustrator, or free alternatives like GIMP and Canva for designing your channel art and logo.
- **Templates and Mockups:** Many online resources offer templates and mockups specifically for YouTube channel art. These can be a great starting point and help ensure your design fits perfectly.

6. Test and Refine

- **Preview on Multiple Devices:** Check how your channel art looks on different devices (desktop, mobile, TV) to ensure it's optimized for all formats.
- **Gather Feedback:** Share your designs with friends, family, or online communities for feedback. Use constructive criticism to refine your designs.
- **A/B Testing:** If possible, experiment with different designs to see which resonates best with your audience. Pay attention to metrics like viewer retention and subscriber growth.

7. Consistency Across Platforms

- **Social Media Integration:** Ensure your branding is consistent across all your social media profiles. Use the same logo, color scheme, and style for a cohesive brand presence.
- **Thumbnails and Video Branding:** Extend your visual branding to video thumbnails, intros, outros, and any on-screen graphics. This reinforces your brand identity and makes your content easily recognizable.

8. Regular Updates

- **Evolve with Your Brand:** As your channel grows and evolves, your branding might need updates. Don't be afraid to refresh your channel art and logo to keep them aligned with your content and audience.
- **Seasonal and Special Themes:** Consider updating your channel art for special occasions, holidays, or significant channel milestones. This can keep your branding fresh and engaging for your audience.

Effective channel art and logos are essential for creating a professional and cohesive brand identity on YouTube. By investing time and effort into designing these elements, you can make a strong first impression, enhance brand recognition, and foster a loyal audience.

Consistent Branding Across All Videos

Ensuring consistent branding across all your videos is vital for creating a strong, recognizable presence on YouTube. This consistency helps to reinforce your brand identity, making it easier for viewers to identify and connect with your content. Here's a detailed guide to help you achieve consistent branding across all your videos:

1. Develop a Signature Intro and Outro

- **Intro:** Create a short, engaging intro that includes your logo, channel name, and a tagline or theme music. Keep it under 10 seconds to retain viewer attention.
- **Outro:** Design an outro that features a call-to-action (CTA) for subscribing, watching other videos, or following on social media. Include your logo and a consistent end screen design.

2. Design Branded Thumbnails

- **Template:** Develop a thumbnail template that includes your brand colors, fonts, and a consistent layout. This helps viewers instantly recognize your videos in their feed.
- **Text and Imagery:** Use clear, bold text and high-quality images that reflect the video content. Keep text to a minimum and ensure it's legible even at small sizes.

3. Use Consistent On-Screen Graphics

- **Lower Thirds:** Design lower third graphics to introduce yourself, guests, or important information. Use your brand colors and fonts to maintain consistency.
- **Transitions and Animations:** Incorporate branded transitions and animations to keep your videos visually engaging and on-brand.

4. Maintain a Cohesive Color Scheme

- **Brand Colors:** Use your brand's color palette consistently across all video elements, including backgrounds, text, and graphics.
- **Visual Harmony:** Ensure that your colors work well together and enhance the overall aesthetic of your videos.

5. Establish a Consistent Tone and Style

- **Speaking Style:** Develop a consistent on-camera persona and speaking style. Whether it's professional, casual, humorous, or inspirational, ensure it aligns with your brand.
- **Visual Style:** Maintain a consistent visual style, including camera angles, lighting, and editing techniques. This creates a unified look and feel across your content.

6. Incorporate Branded Music and Sound Effects

- **Theme Music:** Choose or create a piece of theme music that reflects your brand's personality. Use it consistently in your intros, outros, and transitions.
- **Sound Effects:** Use branded sound effects to enhance viewer engagement and reinforce your brand identity.

7. Consistent Video Descriptions and Titles

- **Title Format:** Develop a consistent format for your video titles, using keywords and phrases that align with your brand and content strategy.
- **Descriptions:** Write detailed video descriptions that follow a consistent format. Include relevant keywords, a brief summary, and links to your social media, website, and other videos.

8. Regular Upload Schedule

- **Consistency:** Stick to a regular upload schedule to build viewer anticipation and loyalty. Whether it's weekly, bi-weekly, or monthly, choose a frequency you can maintain consistently.
- **Promotions:** Promote your schedule in your videos, on your channel banner, and across your social media platforms.

9. Create Playlists and Series

- Playlists: Organize your videos into playlists based on themes or topics. Use consistent thumbnails and titles for each playlist to create a cohesive look.
- Series: Develop video series with a consistent format and theme. This encourages viewers to watch multiple videos and enhances brand recognition.

10. Engage with Your Audience Consistently

- Commenting Style: Develop a consistent style for responding to comments. Be personable and authentic, reflecting your brand's tone and values.
- Community Posts: Use YouTube's community tab to engage with your audience. Share updates, behind-the-scenes content, and polls in a consistent style that aligns with your brand.

11. Collaborations and Guest Appearances

- Branded Intros: When collaborating with other YouTubers, use your branded intro and outro. This maintains consistency and ensures your branding is present.
- Guest Graphics: Design specific graphics for guest introductions and collaborations that match your overall branding.

Consistent branding goes beyond visual elements and extends to the overall experience you provide for your viewers. This includes the tone of your voice, the style of your content, and even the way you engage with your audience in comments and live streams. By maintaining a consistent approach in these areas, you reinforce your brand identity and create a cohesive narrative that your audience can easily follow and connect with. This familiarity makes your content more appealing and helps build a community of loyal viewers who know what to expect from your channel.

Moreover, consistency in branding helps with algorithmic recognition. Platforms like YouTube reward channels that maintain a regular and consistent presence with better visibility in search results and recommendations. When viewers engage with your content, consistent branding makes it easier for the platform to categorize and suggest your videos to new audiences who have similar interests. This increased visibility can lead to higher view counts, more subscribers, and greater overall growth for your channel.

Finally, a strong and consistent brand identity opens doors for collaborations and sponsorships. Brands and other creators are more likely to partner with channels that have a clear and professional identity. They want to associate with creators who have a loyal and engaged audience.

Chapter 13
Promoting Your Channel

Utilizing Social Media for Promotion

Utilizing social media for promoting your YouTube channel is a powerful strategy that can significantly enhance your reach, engagement, and growth. Here's an in-depth guide on how to effectively leverage various social media platforms to promote your YouTube channel:

1. Choosing the Right Platforms

- **Identify Key Platforms:** Focus on social media platforms where your target audience is most active. Popular options include Facebook, Instagram, Twitter, TikTok, LinkedIn, and Pinterest.
- **Understand Platform Strengths:** Each platform has unique features and audiences. Tailor your content to fit the strengths and user behavior of each platform.

2. Creating Platform-Specific Content

- **Instagram:** Use Instagram Stories and IGTV to share short clips, behind-the-scenes content, and teaser trailers. Utilize Instagram Reels for quick, engaging snippets of your videos.

- **Facebook:** Post full-length videos, create event pages for video premieres, and engage with your audience through Facebook Groups and live streams.
- **Twitter:** Share video links, create engaging threads about your video topics, and use relevant hashtags to reach a broader audience. Participate in trending conversations to increase visibility.
- **TikTok:** Make short, engaging videos that highlight key moments from your YouTube content. Use popular sounds and trends to increase discoverability.
- **LinkedIn:** Share professional or educational content related to your videos. Write articles or posts that delve deeper into your video topics and share them with industry-specific groups.
- **Pinterest:** Create eye-catching pins that link to your YouTube videos. Design attractive thumbnails and pin them to relevant boards to drive traffic from this visual-centric platform.

3. Engaging with Your Audience

- **Respond to Comments:** Actively respond to comments and messages on all your social media platforms. Show appreciation for viewer feedback and foster a sense of community.
- **Interactive Content:** Use polls, Q&A sessions, and live streams to interact with your audience in real-time. This engagement increases viewer loyalty.

- **User-Generated Content:** Encourage your audience to create and share content related to your videos. Feature user-generated content on your social media profiles to boost engagement and build a stronger community.

4. Cross-Promoting Content

- **Teasers and Trailers:** Share short teasers and trailers of your YouTube videos on social media to create anticipation and drive traffic to your channel.
- **Linking and Embedding:** Regularly share direct links to your YouTube videos and embed them in posts. Make it easy for your followers to access your content.
- **Content Repurposing:** Repurpose content from your YouTube videos into different formats suitable for social media, such as infographics, quotes, and short clips.

5. Consistency and Scheduling

- **Regular Posting Schedule:** Maintain a consistent posting schedule on social media to keep your audience engaged. Use social media scheduling tools like Hootsuite, Buffer, or Later to plan and automate your posts.
- **Platform-Specific Timing:** Research the best times to post on each platform to maximize reach and engagement. Tailor your posting schedule to when your audience is most active.

6. Collaborations and Partnerships

- **Influencer Collaborations:** Partner with influencers and creators in your niche. Collaborations can help you tap into new audiences and gain credibility.
- **Cross-Promotions:** Work with other YouTubers to cross-promote each other's channels on social media. Joint giveaways, shout-outs, and guest appearances can attract new subscribers.
- **Sponsored Content:** Create sponsored posts that align with your brand and content. Paid promotions can boost visibility and attract a wider audience.

7. Analyzing Performance

- **Social Media Analytics:** Use built-in analytics tools on each platform to track the performance of your posts. Monitor metrics like engagement, reach, and click-through rates.
- **Adjusting Strategies:** Use insights from your analytics to refine your social media strategies. Focus on the types of content and posting times that yield the best results.
- **Feedback and Adaptation:** Listen to feedback from your audience and adapt your content to better meet their preferences and expectations. Actively seek out comments, suggestions, and criticisms from your audience to understand their needs and interests.

8. Integrating Social Media with Your Channel

- **Social Media Links:** Include links to your social media profiles in your YouTube channel description and video descriptions. Encourage viewers to follow you on social media for more updates.
- **End Screens and Annotations:** Use YouTube's end screens and annotations to promote your social media profiles at the end of your videos.
- **Community Engagement:** Share behind-the-scenes content, updates, and personal insights on social media to create a deeper connection with your audience. Use these platforms to foster a sense of community around your channel.

Conclusion

Effectively utilizing social media for promoting your YouTube channel requires a strategic approach tailored to each platform's strengths and audience behavior.

By creating engaging, platform-specific content, actively interacting with your audience, and analyzing performance metrics, you can significantly enhance your channel's visibility and growth. Consistent, thoughtful social media promotion can turn casual viewers into loyal subscribers and expand your reach across the digital landscape.

Collaborations and Influencer Marketing

Collaborations and influencer marketing are powerful strategies to expand your reach, enhance your credibility, and attract new audiences to your YouTube channel. By working with other creators and leveraging their influence, you can achieve greater visibility and engagement. Here's an in-depth guide on how to effectively implement collaborations and influencer marketing:

1. Identifying Potential Collaborators and Influencers

- **Relevance:** Choose collaborators and influencers whose content and audience align with your niche and target demographic. This ensures that their followers are likely to be interested in your content.
- **Audience Size and Engagement:** Look beyond subscriber counts. Evaluate the engagement rates of potential collaborators' audiences, including likes, comments, and shares, to ensure active and genuine followers.
- **Content Quality:** Partner with creators who produce high-quality content that matches or complements your own standards. This helps maintain your brand's reputation and ensures a seamless collaboration. When selecting partners, assess their previous work for consistency, creativity, and alignment with your brand values.

2. Approaching Collaborators and Influencers

- **Personalized Outreach:** Send personalized messages or emails when approaching potential collaborators. Highlight specific reasons why you believe a collaboration would be mutually beneficial.
- **Clear Proposal:** Outline a clear proposal detailing what the collaboration will entail, the benefits for both parties, and any specific ideas or formats you have in mind.
- Flexibility: Be open to their suggestions and input. Collaborations should be a two-way street where both parties feel comfortable and valued.

3. Types of Collaborations

- **Guest Appearances:** Feature each other in your videos. This can include guest spots, interviews, or co-hosting a video. It helps introduce your audience to new faces and vice versa.
- **Joint Projects:** Create a series or special project together. This can be a mini-series, challenge, or themed content that spans multiple videos.
- **Cross-Promotions:** Promote each other's channels through shout-outs, social media posts, and end screen annotations. This can help drive traffic and new subscribers to both channels.

- **Giveaways and Contests:** Partner on giveaways or contests that encourage viewer participation and engagement. This can attract new subscribers and increase viewer interaction.

4. Influencer Marketing Strategies

- **Sponsored Content:** Collaborate with influencers to create sponsored content that promotes your channel or specific videos. Ensure that the content feels authentic and aligns with the influencer's usual style.
- **Product Placements:** If applicable, incorporate your products or services into influencer content. This can be particularly effective if the influencer's audience matches your target market.
- **Affiliate Partnerships:** Set up affiliate marketing arrangements where influencers earn a commission for driving traffic or sales to your channel or products. This incentivizes influencers to promote your content actively.

5. Maximizing Collaboration Impact

- **Cross-Promote on Social Media:** Share the collaboration on all your social media platforms. Encourage your collaborator to do the same to maximize reach.

- **Engage with the New Audience:** Actively engage with new viewers who come from the collaboration. Respond to their comments, welcome them to your channel, and encourage them to explore more of your content.
- **Leverage Email Lists:** If you have an email list, inform your subscribers about the collaboration and encourage them to check it out. This can drive initial traffic and engagement.

6. Measuring Success and ROI

- **Track Performance Metrics:** Use YouTube Analytics and social media insights to track the performance of your collaborative efforts. Key metrics include views, watch time, subscriber growth, and engagement rates.
- **Monitor Referral Traffic:** Use tools like Google Analytics to monitor referral traffic from your collaborator's channels and social media profiles.
- **Evaluate Engagement:** Assess the quality of engagement from the collaboration. Look at comments, shares, and likes to gauge how well the content resonated with viewers.

7. Building Long-Term Relationships

- **Follow-Up:** After the collaboration, follow up with your collaborator to express gratitude and discuss any potential future projects. Maintain a positive and professional relationship.

- **Ongoing Interactions:** Continue interacting with your collaborators on social media and engage with their content. This helps keep the relationship strong and opens doors for future collaborations.
- **Network Expansion:** Use successful collaborations as a stepping stone to network with other influencers and creators. A strong network can lead to more opportunities and growth for your channel.

8. Common Pitfalls to Avoid

- **Misaligned Audiences:** Ensure that the collaborator's audience aligns with your target demographic. Collaborations with unrelated niches can lead to low engagement and minimal benefits.
- **Lack of Clear Communication:** Miscommunication can lead to misunderstandings and unmet expectations. Clearly outline roles, responsibilities, and expectations from the start.
- **Overemphasis on Quantity Over Quality:** Focus on building meaningful, high-quality collaborations rather than numerous low-impact ones. Quality partnerships yield better long-term results.

Collaborations and influencer marketing are essential strategies for growing your YouTube channel. By carefully selecting relevant partners, creating authentic and engaging content.

Paid Advertising on YouTube

Paid advertising on YouTube is a powerful way to reach a larger audience, increase brand awareness, and drive traffic to your channel or website. By leveraging YouTube's vast user base and sophisticated targeting options, you can create effective ad campaigns that yield significant returns. Here's an in-depth guide on how to effectively utilize paid advertising on YouTube:

1. Understanding YouTube Ad Formats

- **TrueView Ads:** These are skippable ads that play before, during, or after a video. You only pay when viewers watch at least 30 seconds or interact with the ad. They are ideal for longer, more detailed messages.
    - **In-Stream Ads:** Play before or during a video and can be skipped after 5 seconds. Best for reaching viewers with a comprehensive message.
    - **Video Discovery Ads:** Appear on YouTube search results and related videos. Effective for attracting viewers to your channel or specific videos.
- **Non-Skippable In-Stream Ads:** These ads must be watched before the viewer can watch their selected video. They are usually 15-20 seconds long and are charged per impression.

- **Bumper Ads:** Non-skippable ads that are up to 6 seconds long. These are great for delivering short, impactful messages and increasing brand recall.
- **Overlay Ads:** Semi-transparent ads that appear on the lower 20% of the video. They are less intrusive and work well for call-to-actions without interrupting the viewer's experience.
- **Sponsored Cards:** Display content relevant to your video, such as products featured in the video. They appear as a teaser for a few seconds and can be expanded by the viewer.

2. Setting Up Your Campaign

- **Google Ads Account:** Create a Google Ads account if you don't have one. This will be your platform for creating and managing YouTube ad campaigns.
- **Campaign Goals:** Define clear goals for your campaign, such as increasing views, driving traffic to your website, boosting subscriptions, or promoting a product or event.
- **Budget and Bidding:** Set a daily or total budget for your campaign to effectively manage your advertising spend and ensure you do not exceed your financial limits. Choose a bidding strategy that aligns with your campaign goals, such as cost-per-view (CPV) if you are aiming for direct engagement, or cost-per-thousand-impressions (CPM) if brand visibility is your primary objective.

3. Targeting Your Audience

- **Demographic Targeting:** Specify the age, gender, and parental status of your target audience.
- **Geographic Targeting:** Choose the locations where you want your ads to appear. This can be as broad as countries or as specific as cities or postal codes.
- **Interests and Behaviors:** Target users based on their interests, habits, and behaviors, such as what videos they watch or their online activity.
- **Custom Affinity Audiences:** Create audiences based on specific interests or activities, allowing for more tailored targeting.
- **Remarketing:** Target users who have previously interacted with your videos or channel. This is effective for re-engaging viewers who are already familiar with your brand.

4. Creating Effective Ad Content

- **Compelling Storytelling:** Craft a narrative that resonates with your target audience. Use strong visuals, clear messaging, and a compelling call-to-action.
- **High-Quality Production:** Ensure your ad is professionally produced with high-quality audio and visuals. Poor production quality can detract from your message and reduce engagement.

- **Engaging Thumbnails:** Design eye-catching thumbnails that encourage clicks and views. Thumbnails should be clear, visually appealing, and representative of the ad content.
- **Clear Call-to-Action:** Include a clear and compelling call-to-action (CTA) in your ad, guiding viewers on what to do next, whether it's visiting your website, subscribing to your channel, or purchasing a product.

5. Optimizing Ad Performance

- **A/B Testing:** Run multiple versions of your ad to see which performs better. Test different elements such as headlines, CTAs, visuals, and ad formats.
- **Monitor Metrics:** Regularly review key metrics such as views, click-through rates (CTR), conversion rates, and cost-per-conversion. Use these insights to refine your campaign.
- **Adjust Targeting:** Optimize your audience targeting based on performance data. Narrow down or expand your audience to improve engagement and ROI.
- **Refine Messaging:** Continuously refine your ad messaging to better align with your audience's interests and responses. Use feedback and performance data to guide improvements. Analyzing metrics such as click-through rates, conversion rates, and audience engagement can provide valuable insights into what resonates with your audience.

6. Measuring Campaign Succes

- **Key Performance Indicators (KPIs):** Define KPIs based on your campaign goals. Common KPIs include view count, average watch time, CTR, conversion rates, and return on ad spend (ROAS).
- **Google Analytics:** Integrate Google Analytics to track user behavior on your website or channel after interacting with your ads. This provides deeper insights into ad performance and user engagement.
- **Attribution Models:** Use attribution models to understand the customer journey and the role of your YouTube ads in driving conversions. This helps in allocating budget more effectively across different marketing channels.

7. Utilizing Advanced Strategies

- **Lookalike Audiences:** Create lookalike audiences based on your existing viewers or subscribers. This helps you reach new potential viewers who share similar characteristics with your current audience.
- **Sequential Advertising:** Use sequential advertising to tell a story over multiple ads. This strategy can guide viewers through a funnel, from awareness to consideration to conversion.

- Ad Extensions: Utilize ad extensions like site links, callouts, and structured snippets to provide additional information and enhance the visibility of your ads.

8. Leveraging YouTube's Tools and Resources

- **YouTube Studio:** Use YouTube Studio to manage your channel, review performance analytics, and gain insights into your audience's behavior and preferences.
- **Creator Academy:** Take advantage of YouTube's Creator Academy to learn best practices, tips, and strategies for creating and optimizing ads.
- **Google Support and Community:** Utilize Google's support resources and community forums to troubleshoot issues, share experiences, and learn from other advertisers.

Paid advertising on YouTube offers a robust platform to amplify your reach, drive engagement, and achieve your marketing goals. By understanding the various ad formats, setting up targeted campaigns, creating compelling content, and continuously optimizing your strategies, you can maximize the impact of your YouTube ads. Investing in paid advertising not only helps in gaining immediate visibility but also contributes to long-term growth and success for your channel or brand.

Chapter 14
Leveraging Trends and Viral Content

Identifying Trending Topics

Identifying trending topics is crucial for creating relevant, timely, and engaging content that resonates with your audience and attracts new viewers. Staying on top of current trends helps keep your content fresh and increases the likelihood of your videos being discovered. Here's a comprehensive guide on how to effectively identify and leverage trending topics:

1. Using YouTube Tools and Features

- **YouTube Trending Tab:** Regularly check the Trending tab on YouTube to see which videos and topics are currently popular. This can give you insights into what's capturing the audience's attention.
- **YouTube Analytics:** Use YouTube Analytics to monitor the performance of your videos and see which topics have historically performed well. Look for patterns and capitalize on popular themes.
- **YouTube Search Autocomplete:** Start typing keywords related to your niche in the YouTube search bar and pay attention to the autocomplete suggestions. These are often based on popular searches.

2. Leveraging Google Trends

- **Explore Topics:** Use Google Trends to explore the popularity of different search terms over time. You can filter results by region, time frame, and category to find the most relevant trends.
- **Related Queries:** Look at related queries to see what other topics people are searching for in connection with your main keyword. This can help you uncover emerging trends.
- **Trending Searches:** Check the Trending Searches section to see what's currently gaining traction. This can provide you with immediate inspiration for timely content.

3. Monitoring Social Media Platforms

- **Twitter Trends:** Follow Twitter's trending topics to see what people are talking about in real-time. This can give you a pulse on current events and popular discussions.
- **Hashtags and Challenges:** Pay attention to trending hashtags and challenges on platforms like Instagram, TikTok, and Facebook. Participating in popular trends can increase your content's visibility.
- **Reddit:** Explore subreddits related to your niche. Reddit is a treasure trove of user-generated content and discussions that can highlight what's trending in specific communities.

4. Engaging with Your Audience

- **Polls and Surveys:** Conduct polls and surveys on your YouTube community tab or social media platforms to ask your audience what topics they are interested in.
- **Comment Section:** Pay attention to the comments on your videos and other popular videos in your niche. Viewers often express what they want to see more of.
- **Live Q&A Sessions:** Host live Q&A sessions to interact directly with your audience. These sessions can provide immediate feedback and insights into trending topics.

5. Following Industry News and Influencers

- **News Websites:** Regularly read news websites, blogs, and industry publications related to your niche. This keeps you informed about the latest developments and trends.
- **Influencer Content:** Follow influencers and thought leaders in your industry. See what they are talking about and how their audience is reacting. This can provide inspiration and validate trending topics.
- **Industry Events:** Stay updated with major industry events, conferences, and product launches. These events often generate buzz and can become trending topics.

6. Utilizing Content Research Tools

- **BuzzSumo:** Use BuzzSumo to discover the most shared content on social media across various topics. This tool can help you identify what's currently resonating with audiences.
- **AnswerThePublic:** This tool generates a list of questions and phrases that people are searching for related to your keyword. It's useful for identifying trending questions and concerns.
- **Feedly:** Set up a Feedly account to aggregate RSS feeds from your favorite blogs, news sites, and YouTube channels. This helps you stay on top of new content and emerging trends in one place.

7. Collaborating and Networking

- **Join Online Communities:** Participate in online communities and forums related to your niche. Engaging in discussions can provide insights into what's trending among passionate members.
- **Collaboration Opportunities:** Collaborate with other YouTubers and content creators. Joint projects can expose you to new audiences and trending topics that you might not have considered.
- **Webinars and Podcasts:** Attend webinars and listen to podcasts in your industry. Hosts and speakers often discuss current trends and future predictions.

8. Seasonal and Event-Based Trends

- **Calendar Events:** Plan content around major holidays, seasons, and events. These times often come with built-in trends and increased search activity.
- **Annual Trends:** Identify recurring trends that happen every year in your niche. For example, fitness channels can capitalize on New Year's resolutions, while tech channels can focus on product launches.

9. Analyzing Competitor Content

- **Competitor Channels:** Monitor the content of your competitors to see what topics they are covering and how well those videos are performing.
- **Gap Analysis:** Identify content gaps where trending topics haven't been extensively covered by your competitors. This gives you an opportunity to fill those gaps and attract viewers.

10. Creating Timely and Evergreen Content

- **Timely Content:** Produce content that taps into current trends and events. This can attract immediate attention and boost your visibility.
- **Evergreen Content:** Balance timely content with evergreen topics that remain relevant over time.

Identifying trending topics requires a proactive approach and the use of various tools and strategies. By staying informed through platforms like YouTube, Google Trends, and social media, you can monitor what is currently capturing the public's interest.

Engaging with your audience through comments, polls, and direct interactions provides insights into their preferences and emerging trends. Following industry news and developments keeps you updated on the latest happenings that may interest your audience. Analyzing competitor content can also reveal trends that are gaining traction and help you identify gaps or opportunities to differentiate your content.

Leveraging trending topics not only boosts your visibility and engagement but also helps establish your channel as a go-to source for timely and valuable content. By consistently producing videos that resonate with current interests, you can attract a larger audience and foster a community of loyal viewers.

This approach enhances your credibility and authority in your niche, making your channel more appealing to both new and existing subscribers. Additionally, staying ahead of trends allows you to capitalize on search engine optimization (SEO) benefits, as timely and relevant content is more likely to be discovered and shared.

Creating Viral-Ready Content

Creating viral-ready content involves crafting videos that have a high potential to be widely shared and viewed, maximizing your reach and impact. While there's no guaranteed formula for virality, there are certain strategies and elements you can incorporate to increase your chances of creating content that resonates with a large audience. Here's an in-depth guide on how to create viral-ready content:

1. Understanding Your Audience

- **Know Your Demographic:** Identify the interests, preferences, and pain points of your target audience. Tailor your content to address their needs and capture their attention.
- **Analyze Viewer Behavior:** Use YouTube Analytics to study your audience's viewing patterns, engagement rates, and feedback. Understand what type of content they enjoy and why.

2. Compelling Storytelling

- **Emotional Connection:** Create content that evokes strong emotions, whether it's happiness, surprise, sadness, or excitement. Emotional content is more likely to be shared.
- **Relatable Narratives:** Share stories or scenarios that your audience can relate to.

- **Clear Structure:** Ensure your video has a clear beginning, middle, and end. A well-structured story keeps viewers engaged and makes your message more impactful.

3. Unique and Original Ideas

- **Innovative Concepts:** Think outside the box and come up with unique ideas that stand out. Originality captures attention and distinguishes your content from the competition.
- **Trendy Twists:** Combine trending topics with your unique spin. This can attract viewers interested in the trend while offering them something fresh and different.
- **Niche Appeal:** Sometimes, highly specific content can go viral within a particular community or niche. Tap into niche interests and create highly targeted content.

4. High-Quality Production

- **Professional Quality:** Invest in good equipment for filming and editing. High-quality visuals and audio make your content more enjoyable to watch and share.
- **Attention to Detail:** Pay attention to lighting, sound, and overall production quality. Even small improvements can make a significant difference in viewer experience.

- **Editing Skills:** Use engaging editing techniques to maintain viewer interest. Quick cuts, effects, and smooth transitions can enhance the overall appeal of your video.

5. Catchy Titles and Thumbnails

- **Enticing Titles:** Craft compelling titles that pique curiosity and accurately reflect the content. Use keywords to improve discoverability.
- **Eye-Catching Thumbnails:** Design visually appealing thumbnails that stand out. Use bright colors, clear images, and text overlays to attract clicks.
- **Honesty:** Ensure that your titles and thumbnails are not misleading. Disappointment can lead to negative feedback and reduced shares.

6. Engaging Introductions

- **Hook Viewers Early:** Capture attention within the first few seconds of your video. Use a strong hook to entice viewers to keep watching.
- **Preview of Content:** Give a brief overview of what the video will cover. This helps set expectations and keeps viewers interested in seeing more. By providing a sneak peek of the main points or highlights, you can intrigue your audience and encourage them to stay engaged throughout the entire video.

7. Incorporating Trends and Challenges

- **Stay Current:** Keep up with the latest trends, challenges, and memes. Incorporating these into your content can increase relevance and shareability.
- **Creative Adaptations:** Put your unique twist on popular trends. This can help you stand out while still benefiting from the trend's popularity.
- Timeliness: Act quickly on trends. The faster you produce and publish content around a trend, the higher the chances of it going viral.

8. Encouraging Viewer Interaction

- **Calls to Action:** Encourage viewers to like, comment, share, and subscribe. Direct engagement helps boost your video's visibility and chances of going viral.
- **Interactive Elements:** Use polls, questions, and prompts to engage your audience. Interactive content encourages participation and sharing.
- **Community Building:** Foster a sense of community around your content. Engaged communities are more likely to share your videos with others.

9. Optimizing for Social Sharing

- **Shareable Content:** Create content that viewers will want to share with their friends and family. This often includes humor or inspiration.

- **Social Media Integration:** Promote your videos across all your social media platforms. Use platform-specific strategies to maximize reach and engagement.
- **Embed Options:** Enable embedding so your videos can be easily shared on blogs and websites.

10. Consistency and Frequency

- **Regular Posting Schedule:** Maintain a consistent posting schedule to keep your audience engaged and coming back for more.
- **Series and Sequels:** Create content series or follow-ups to popular videos. This keeps viewers invested in your channel and increases the likelihood of sharing.
- **Quality over Quantity:** While frequency is important, never sacrifice quality. High-quality content is more likely to be shared and go viral.

11. Collaborations and Influencer Partnerships

- **Partner with Influencers:** Collaborate with influencers and other creators to tap into their audience. Influencer partnerships can significantly boost your reach and visibility.
- **Guest Appearances:** Feature guests who are popular within your niche. Their followers are likely to watch and share your content.

- **Cross-Promotions:** Engage in cross-promotional activities with other creators. Promote each other's content to expand your audience base.

12. Analyzing and Iterating

- **Performance Metrics:** Regularly analyze your video performance using YouTube Analytics. Track metrics like views, watch time, engagement, and shares.
- **Feedback Loop:** Pay attention to viewer feedback and comments. Use this information to improve your content and address audience preferences.
- **Continuous Improvement:** Experiment with different formats, styles, and topics. Learn from each video and continuously refine your approach.

Creating viral-ready content involves a mix of creativity, strategy, and execution. By understanding your audience, crafting compelling stories, and leveraging high-quality production, you can create videos that have the potential to be widely shared. Stay current with trends, engage with your audience, and optimize your content for social sharing to maximize your chances of going viral. While there are no guarantees, these strategies can significantly enhance your ability to create impactful, shareable content that resonates with a broad audience.

Timing Your Uploads for Maximum Impact

Timing your uploads for maximum impact is a crucial aspect of maximizing your video's reach and engagement. Posting videos at the right times can significantly enhance visibility, viewer engagement, and overall channel growth. Here's an in-depth guide on how to effectively time your uploads for maximum impact:

1. Understanding Your Audience's Habits

- **Analyze Viewer Data:** Use YouTube Analytics to study when your audience is most active. Look at metrics like peak view times, days of the week, and time zones.
- **Demographic Insights:** Consider the age, location, and lifestyle of your target audience. For example, students might have different viewing habits compared to working professionals.
- **Engagement Patterns:** Identify patterns in your engagement metrics. Are there certain times when your videos receive more likes, comments, and shares?

2. Optimal Days and Times

- **General Best Practices:** While specific optimal times vary by audience, some general best practices include:

- **Weekdays:** Posting on weekdays, particularly from Tuesday to Thursday, can yield good results.
- **Weekends:** Depending on your audience, weekends can also be effective, especially for leisure and entertainment content.

- **Time of Day:** Consider the following time slots, adjusted for your audience's time zone:

    - **Early Morning (6-9 AM):** Capture viewers starting their day.
    - **Mid-Morning (9-12 PM):** Reach audiences during work breaks.
    - **Afternoon (12-3 PM):** Engage viewers during lunch breaks.
    - **Evening (5-8 PM):** Ideal for after-work relaxation and viewing.
    - **Late Evening (8-11 PM):** Target night owls and viewers winding down for the day.

3. Leveraging Time Zones

- **Global Audience:** If your channel has a global audience, consider time zones across different regions. You may need to stagger uploads or schedule posts to cater to multiple time zones.
- **Primary Audience Location:** Focus on the time zone where the majority of your audience is located. This ensures that most of your viewers receive notifications at an optimal time.

4. Scheduling Consistency

- **Regular Upload Schedule:** Establish a consistent upload schedule. Regular posting builds anticipation and routine among your viewers, leading to higher engagement.
- **Weekly Series:** Consider creating a weekly series or special segments that air on the same day and time each week. This can create a loyal viewership who tune in regularly.

5. Seasonal and Event-Based Timing

- **Holidays and Events:** Align your content with holidays, seasons, and significant events. Posting themed content around these times can attract more viewers.
- **Special Occasions:** Take advantage of special occasions related to your niche, such as product launches, anniversaries, or industry events.

6. Analyzing Competitor Strategies

- **Competitor Uploads:** Study the upload schedules of successful competitors in your niche. Identify patterns and see if there are common times when they post their videos.
- **Content Gaps:** Look for gaps in competitors' schedules where there's less content being posted. Filling these gaps can help you capture more attention.

7. Testing and Iteration

- **Experiment with Timing:** Conduct experiments by posting videos at different times and days. Track the performance of each upload to identify what works best for your audience.
- **A/B Testing:** Use A/B testing to compare the performance of videos posted at different times. This data-driven approach can help refine your upload schedule.
- Monitor Analytics: Continuously monitor your YouTube Analytics for insights. Adjust your strategy based on performance metrics and viewer feedback.

8. Utilizing YouTube Premieres

- **Premiere Feature:** Use YouTube's Premiere feature to schedule your video releases. Premiering videos can build anticipation and create a live viewing experience with real-time chat.
- **Promote Premieres:** Promote your scheduled premieres across social media and your YouTube community tab. Encourage viewers to set reminders and join the premiere event.

9. Engaging with Viewers Post-Upload

- **Immediate Interaction:** Be available to engage with viewers in the comments section immediately after uploading.

- **Community Posts:** Use community posts to remind your audience about your new upload. This can drive additional traffic to your video shortly after it goes live.

10. Optimizing for YouTube Algorithm

- **Algorithm Signals:** Uploading at optimal times can help trigger YouTube's algorithm to promote your content. Higher initial engagement (views, likes, comments) can increase the likelihood of your video being recommended.
- **Watch Time:** Focus on maximizing watch time by creating engaging content. Higher watch time signals to YouTube that your video is valuable, further boosting its visibility.

11. Leveraging Social Media

- **Cross-Promotion:** Promote your videos on all your social media platforms at the time of upload. This can drive immediate traffic and boost engagement.
- **Timing Consistency:** Align your social media promotion schedule with your YouTube upload schedule to ensure maximum impact and viewer awareness. Consistently promoting your videos across various social media platforms at the same time they are uploaded to YouTube helps create a synchronized marketing effort that can significantly boost visibility and engagement.

Chapter 15
Utilizing YouTube Tools and Plugins

Recommended Tools for Content Creators

Content creators have access to a wide array of tools designed to enhance productivity, improve content quality, and streamline the creation process. Utilizing the right tools can make a significant difference in the efficiency and effectiveness of your work. Here's an expanded guide on recommended tools for content creators, covering various aspects of content creation:

1. Video Editing Software

- **Adobe Premiere Pro:** A professional-grade video editing software with extensive features for precise editing, color correction, and special effects.
- **Final Cut Pro:** A powerful video editing tool for Mac users, known for its advanced features and smooth performance.
- **DaVinci Resolve:** Offers professional video editing, color grading, and audio post-production capabilities, available in both free and paid versions.
- **iMovie:** A user-friendly video editing software for Mac users, suitable for beginners and intermediate creators.

2. Graphic Design Tools

- **Adobe Photoshop:** The industry standard for image editing and graphic design, offering a wide range of features for creating high-quality visuals.
- **Canva:** A web-based design tool that provides templates and easy-to-use design elements, ideal for creating social media graphics, thumbnails, and more.
- **GIMP:** A free, open-source image editor that offers advanced photo retouching and image composition tools.
- **Affinity Photo:** A cost-effective alternative to Photoshop, offering professional-grade photo editing capabilities.

3. Audio Editing Software

- **Adobe Audition:** A comprehensive audio editing tool for recording, mixing, and mastering audio with precision.
- **Audacity:** A free, open-source audio editing software with a wide range of features for recording and editing sound.
- **GarageBand:** A beginner-friendly audio editing tool for Mac users, suitable for creating music, podcasts, and voiceovers.
- **Reaper:** A powerful and affordable digital audio workstation (DAW) that supports multi-track recording and editing.

4. Screen Recording and Streaming Tools

- **OBS Studio:** A free, open-source software for video recording and live streaming, widely used by gamers and content creators.
- **Camtasia:** A user-friendly screen recording and video editing tool, ideal for creating tutorials, presentations, and instructional videos.
- **Streamlabs OBS:** An enhanced version of OBS Studio with additional features for streamers, including customizable alerts and overlays.
- **XSplit Broadcaster:** A professional live streaming and recording software with advanced features for stream management.

5. Content Planning and Management

- **Trello:** A visual project management tool that uses boards, lists, and cards to help you organize and prioritize your content creation tasks.
- **Asana:** A task management tool that allows you to plan, organize, and track your content creation projects and deadlines.
- **Notion:** An all-in-one workspace for note-taking, project management, and collaboration, suitable for organizing content ideas and workflows.
- **Google Calendar:** A simple and effective tool for scheduling content uploads, deadlines, and collaboration meetings.

6. SEO and Analytics Tools

- **TubeBuddy:** A browser extension that provides keyword research, SEO optimization, and analytics tools specifically for YouTube creators.
- **vidIQ:** Another browser extension offering insights into video performance, keyword research, and competitor analysis for YouTube.
- **Google Analytics:** A powerful tool for tracking website traffic, user behavior, and conversion rates, useful for content creators with blogs or websites.
- **SEMrush:** An all-in-one marketing toolkit that offers SEO, PPC, content marketing, and competitive research tools.

7. Social Media Management

- **Hootsuite:** A comprehensive social media management tool that allows you to schedule posts, track engagement, and manage multiple social media accounts.
- **Buffer:** A user-friendly tool for scheduling social media posts, analyzing performance, and managing multiple accounts.
- **Later:** A visual content calendar for planning and scheduling Instagram posts, including a drag-and-drop feature for easy organization.
- **Sprout Social:** A robust platform for managing social media campaigns, monitoring engagement, and analyzing .

8. Collaboration and Communication Tools

- **Slack:** A team communication tool that offers channels, direct messaging, and integrations with other tools to streamline collaboration.
- **Microsoft Teams:** A collaboration platform that combines chat, video meetings, and file storage, ideal for remote content creation teams.
- **Zoom:** A video conferencing tool that allows for virtual meetings, webinars, and screen sharing, useful for team collaboration and interviews.
- **Google Drive:** A cloud storage service that allows you to store, share, and collaborate on documents, spreadsheets, and presentations.

9. Thumbnail and Banner Creation

- **Snappa:** A graphic design tool that simplifies the creation of thumbnails, social media graphics, and banners with pre-made templates.
- **PicMonkey:** An online design tool for creating eye-catching thumbnails, banners, and social media posts with ease.
- **Crello:** A design platform offering templates and design elements for creating professional-looking thumbnails and graphics.
- **Adobe Spark:** A tool for creating graphics, web pages, and video stories, suitable for designing engaging thumbnails and banners.

10. Content Ideation and Research

- **AnswerThePublic:** A tool that visualizes search queries and helps you discover what people are asking about your topic, providing valuable content ideas.
- **BuzzSumo:** Analyzes the most shared content across social media platforms, helping you identify trending topics and popular content formats.
- **Quora:** A question-and-answer platform where you can discover common questions and interests in your niche, generating content ideas.
- **Google Trends:** A tool that shows the popularity of search queries over time, helping you identify trending topics and seasonality in your content.

Conclusion

Choosing the right tools can greatly enhance your content creation process, from ideation and planning to production and promotion. By leveraging these recommended tools, you can streamline your workflow, improve the quality of your content, and effectively reach and engage your audience. Whether you're a beginner or an experienced creator, investing in the right tools can help you achieve your content creation goals and grow your online presence.

Plugins for Enhanced SEO

Enhanced SEO for YouTube can significantly improve your video visibility, engagement, and overall channel growth. Utilizing plugins and tools specifically designed for YouTube SEO can help you optimize your videos for better search rankings and attract a larger audience. Here's an in-depth guide on some of the most effective YouTube SEO plugins and tools:

1. TubeBuddy

- **Features:**
    - **Keyword Explorer:** Helps you find the best keywords for your videos by providing search volume, competition, and related keywords.
    - **Tag Suggestions:** Suggests tags that can improve your video's discoverability.
    - **SEO Studio:** Guides you through optimizing your video title, description, tags, and thumbnail.
    - **Bulk Processing Tools:** Allows bulk updates for end screens, cards, annotations, and descriptions.
    - **Competitor Analysis:** Tracks your competitors' strategies and performance, offering insights into how to improve your own content.
    - **A/B Testing:** Tests different thumbnails, titles, and descriptions.

- **Benefits:**
  - **Comprehensive:** Covers a wide range of SEO aspects, from keyword research to competitor analysis.
  - **User-Friendly:** Easy to navigate with actionable insights and recommendations.

2. vidIQ

- **Features:**
  - **Keyword Research:** Provides in-depth keyword insights, including search volume, competition, and related terms.
  - **Tag Recommendations:** Suggests relevant tags to maximize your video's visibility.
  - **SEO Score:** Analyzes your video's SEO score and offers recommendations for improvement.
  - **Competitor Tracking:** Monitors your competitors' videos and channels to help you stay ahead.
  - **Trend Alerts:** Alerts you to trending topics in your niche, helping you create timely content.
  - **Channel Audit:** Provides a comprehensive audit of your channel's performance, highlighting areas for improvement.

- **Benefits:**
  - Analytics-Driven: Offers detailed analytics and insights to help you make data-driven decisions.

- **Performance Monitoring:** Tracks your video's performance and offers actionable tips to boost visibility.

3. Morningfame

- **Features:**
    - **Keyword Research:** Provides keyword suggestions and metrics to help you find the best keywords for your videos.
    - **Video Optimization:** Guides you through optimizing your video title, description, tags, and thumbnail for better SEO.
    - **Performance Tracking:** Tracks your video's performance and provides insights into what's working and what's not.
    - **Growth Recommendations:** Offers personalized recommendations to help you grow your channel.
- **Benefits:**
    - **Easy-to-Use:** Simple interface with step-by-step guides for beginners.
    - **Personalized Insights:** Tailored recommendations based on your channel's performance and goals.

4. SEO Stack Keyword Tool

- **Features:**
    - **Keyword Research:** Generates a list of relevant keywords.

- **Competitor Analysis:** Analyzes your competitors' videos and channels to identify successful keywords and strategies.
  - Long-Tail Keywords: Helps you find long-tail keywords to target less competitive niches.

- **Benefits:**
  - **Detailed Insights:** Provides comprehensive data on keyword performance.
  - **Competitor Benchmarking:** Allows you to compare your SEO efforts with those of your competitors.

5. Keywords Everywhere

- **Features:**
  - **Keyword Metrics:** Provides search volume, cost-per-click (CPC), and competition data for keywords on YouTube and other platforms.
  - **Related Keywords:** Suggests related keywords to help you expand your reach.
  - **Trend Analysis:** Shows trending keywords to help you create timely and relevant content.

- **Benefits:**
  - **Cross-Platform:** Works across multiple platforms, including YouTube, Google, and Bing.
  - **Cost-Effective:** Offers valuable keyword insights at an affordable price.

6. TubeRanker

- **Features:**
  - **Keyword Research:** Helps you find the best keywords for your videos to improve search rankings.
  - **Video Optimization:** Provides tools and tips for optimizing your video titles, descriptions, and tags.
  - **Rank Tracking:** Tracks your video rankings for specific keywords over time.
  - **SEO Reports:** Generates detailed SEO reports for your videos and channel.

- **Benefits:**
  - **Focused Tools:** Specializes in YouTube SEO, offering targeted insights and recommendations.
  - **Performance Monitoring:** Helps you keep track of your SEO progress and make necessary adjustments.

7. RapidTags

- **Features:**
  - Tag Generator: Quickly generates relevant tags for your videos based on your main keyword.
  - SEO Analysis: Provides basic SEO analysis and recommendations for your video content.

- **Benefits:**
  - **Efficiency:** Saves time by generating tags instantly.
  - **Simplicity:** Easy to use with a straightforward interface.

8. Social Blade

- **Features:**
  - **Channel Analytics:** Provides detailed statistics and insights for your YouTube channel.
  - **Competitor Analysis:** Tracks competitors' channels and videos to offer comparative insights.
  - **Trend Analysis:** Identifies trends in your niche to help you create relevant content.
  - **Growth Metrics:** Offers projections for your channel's future growth based on current performance.

- **Benefits:**
  - **Comprehensive Analytics:** Provides a wide range of data to help you understand and improve your channel's performance.
  - **Competitor Insights:** Helps you stay ahead by analyzing competitors' strategies and success.

9. Canva

- **Features:**
  - **Thumbnail Creation:** Provides customizable templates and design tools for creating eye-catching YouTube thumbnails.
  - **Banner Design:** Helps you design professional-looking YouTube banners to enhance your channel's branding.
  - **Social Media Graphics:** Offers tools for creating graphics to promote your videos across social media platforms.
- **Benefits:**
  - **User-Friendly:** Easy to use with a drag-and-drop interface.
  - **Professional Designs:** Provides high-quality templates and design elements to improve your visual branding.

10. TuberTools

- **Features:**
  - **Graphics Library:** Offers a library of pre-made graphics, including thumbnails, banners, and social media posts.
  - **End Screens and Cards:** Provides templates and tools for creating engaging end screens and cards.
  - **Channel Branding:** Includes tools for designing logos, watermarks, and other branding elements.

- **Benefits:**
- **Customization:** Allows you to customize templates to match your channel's branding.
- **Professional Quality:** Offers high-quality graphics to enhance your channel's visual appeal.

These tools offer more than just basic SEO optimization. They empower creators to delve into detailed analytics, identifying which keywords resonate most with their audience and competitors. This insight allows for strategic adjustments in video titles, descriptions, and tags to maximize discoverability and viewer engagement.

Additionally, plugins like TubeBuddy and vidIQ provide comprehensive competitor analysis, offering visibility into their strategies and performance metrics. This competitive intelligence enables creators to fine-tune their content strategies, capitalize on emerging trends, and differentiate their channels effectively.

Moreover, the ability to create compelling visuals through tools like Canva and TuberTools enhances a channel's professional image and viewer appeal. High-quality thumbnails and channel art not only attract initial clicks but also contribute to higher retention rates and subscriber growth.

Chapter 16
Legal and Ethical Considerations

Copyright and Fair Use

As the world's largest video-sharing platform, YouTube has become a hub for creators and consumers alike. However, with its vast library of content, copyright issues often arise. Understanding copyright and fair use is essential for anyone looking to create and share content on YouTube.

Understanding Copyright

Copyright is a legal framework that gives creators of original works exclusive rights to their creations. This includes works like music, videos, books, and more. On YouTube, copyright issues most commonly arise with the use of music, clips from movies or TV shows, and other content created by someone else.

Copyright Infringement

When you upload a video to YouTube, you need to ensure that all elements of the content (video, audio, images, etc.) are either original or used with permission.

Uploading content that you do not own or do not have permission to use can result in a copyright claim or strike against your account. Repeated violations can lead to account suspension or termination.

Content ID

YouTube uses a system called Content ID to identify and manage copyrighted content. When you upload a video, Content ID scans it against a database of copyrighted works. If a match is found, the copyright owner can choose to monetize the video, block it, or track its viewership statistics.

Fair Use Doctrine

Fair use is a legal doctrine that allows limited use of copyrighted material without permission from the owner, under certain conditions. It is designed to balance the interests of copyright holders with the public's interest in free expression and the dissemination of information.

Factors of Fair Use

There are four factors that determine whether a use is considered fair:

- **Purpose and Character of the Use:** Non-commercial, educational, or transformative.

- **Nature of the Copyrighted Work:** Using factual works is more likely to be fair use than using highly creative works.
- **Amount and Substantiality:** Using smaller portions of a work may be more likely to be considered fair use, especially if the portion used is not the "heart" of the work.
- **Effect on the Market:** If the use of the work negatively impacts its market value or potential sales, it is less likely to be considered fair use.

Examples of Fair Use on YouTube

- **Commentary and Criticism:** Reviewing a movie or video game and including short clips to illustrate points.
- **Parody:** Creating a humorous or satirical imitation of a copyrighted work.
- **Educational Use:** Using short clips from a documentary in an educational video.

Best Practices for YouTube Creators

- **Create Original Content:** The safest way to avoid copyright issues is to create content that is entirely your own.
- **Get Permission:** If you want to use someone else's work, seek permission or a license to use it.
- **Use Royalty-Free or Creative Commons Content:** There are many resources available for royalty-free music, images, and videos.

- **Understand Fair Use:** If you believe your use of copyrighted material falls under fair use, be prepared to explain how it meets the criteria.
- **Provide Attribution:** Even when using content that is allowed under Creative Commons or other licenses, always give proper credit to the original creator.

Handling Copyright Claims

If you receive a copyright claim on YouTube, you have a few options:

- **Accept the Claim:** If you agree with the claim, you can accept it, and the copyright owner may choose to monetize the video.
- **Remove or Replace Content:** You can remove the claimed content or use YouTube's tools to replace the music or edit the video.
- **Dispute the Claim:** If you believe the claim is incorrect, you can dispute it. Be prepared to provide evidence supporting your use of the material.

Understanding copyright and fair use is crucial for any YouTube creator. By following best practices and staying informed, you can protect your channel from copyright issues and continue to share your creative work with the world. In addition to safeguarding your content, understanding these principles also empowers you to leverage existing works legally and creatively.

Chapter 17
Case Studies of Successful Channels

Lessons Learned from Top YouTubers

Lessons learned from top YouTubers can provide invaluable insights into building and sustaining a successful YouTube channel. By analyzing their strategies, content, and audience engagement tactics, you can adopt proven methods to enhance your channel's growth. Here's an in-depth guide on some of the key lessons learned from top YouTubers:

1. Consistency is Key

- **Regular Upload Schedule:** Top YouTubers like Casey Neistat and PewDiePie emphasize the importance of maintaining a consistent upload schedule. This helps build anticipation and loyalty among viewers.
- **Content Variety:** While consistency in posting is crucial, many successful YouTubers also mix up their content types to keep their audience engaged and attract new viewers. For example, they might alternate between vlogs, tutorials, and live streams. This approach not only prevents the content from becoming monotonous but also caters to different segments of their audience.

2. Authenticity and Relatability

- **Be Genuine:** Audiences can easily spot inauthenticity. Top YouTubers like Emma Chamberlain and David Dobrik have built massive followings by being themselves and sharing their real-life experiences.
- **Engage Personally:** Engaging with your audience on a personal level, through Q&A sessions, reading comments, and responding to fan messages, helps build a strong community.

3. Quality Over Quantity

- **High Production Value:** Creators like Marques Brownlee (MKBHD) focus on producing high-quality content with excellent production value. This involves investing in good equipment, editing software, and taking the time to craft well-thought-out videos.
- **Attention to Detail:** Paying attention to small details like sound quality, lighting, and video editing can significantly enhance viewer experience and retention.

4. Niche Focus

- **Targeted Content:** Successful YouTubers often find a niche they are passionate about and focus on it.

- **Expertise and Authority:** By consistently producing content in a specific niche, top YouTubers build authority and become go-to sources for information and entertainment in that area.

5. Engaging Thumbnails and Titles

- **Eye-Catching Thumbnails:** Creators like MrBeast and Ali-A use vibrant, eye-catching thumbnails that accurately represent the video content, which helps attract clicks.
- **Compelling Titles:** Writing engaging, curiosity-inducing titles is crucial. The title should be relevant to the content but also crafted in a way that piques interest.

6. Leveraging Trends and Challenges

- **Timely Content:** Top YouTubers often jump on trending topics and challenges to capitalize on the increased interest. For instance, participating in viral challenges or creating content around current events can boost visibility.
- **Adaptation:** They adapt to changing trends and algorithms by keeping up with the latest in the YouTube ecosystem and adjusting their content strategies accordingly.

7. Collaboration and Networking

- **Collaborations:** Collaborating with other YouTubers can help tap into new audiences. Creators like Liza Koshy and the Dolan Twins frequently collaborate with peers to expand their reach.
- **Cross-Promotion:** Engaging in cross-promotion with other content creators, social media influencers, and brands helps in gaining exposure to a broader audience.

8. Audience Interaction and Community Building

- **Active Engagement:** Top YouTubers engage with their audience through comments, social media, live chats, and community posts. This interaction helps build a loyal community.
- **Fan Involvement:** Involving fans in content creation, such as through polls, fan art showcases, and shout-outs, enhances viewer loyalty and connection.

9. Monetization Strategies

- **Diverse Revenue Streams:** Successful YouTubers often diversify their income streams through ad revenue, sponsorships, merchandise, memberships, and crowdfunding (e.g., Patreon).

- **Transparency with Sponsored Content:** Being transparent about sponsored content and maintaining a balance between sponsored and organic content helps maintain viewer trust.

10. Continuous Learning and Adaptation

- **Analytical Approach:** Analyzing video performance and audience feedback helps in understanding what works and what doesn't. Top YouTubers use tools like YouTube Analytics to make data-driven decisions.
- **Evolving Content:** They constantly evolve their content to keep it fresh and relevant. This might involve experimenting with new formats, styles, or topics based on audience preferences and trends.

Learning from top YouTubers involves more than just replicating their content style; it requires understanding the principles and strategies behind their success. By focusing on consistency, authenticity, quality, niche expertise, and active audience engagement, you can create a compelling channel that attracts and retains viewers.

Adapting these lessons to fit your unique voice and content will help you navigate the competitive landscape of YouTube and achieve long-term growth.

In closing, this book has explored a myriad of strategies and insights aimed at empowering you as a content creator on YouTube. From mastering SEO techniques and engaging with your audience to leveraging trends and refining your content strategy, the journey to success on YouTube is both challenging and rewarding. Remember, consistency, authenticity, and continuous adaptation are key pillars of growth. As you embark on your YouTube journey, may these principles guide you towards building a thriving channel that not only captures attention but also fosters lasting connections with your viewers. Here's to your continued success in the vibrant world of online video content.

Throughout these pages, we've delved into the essential tools and strategies needed to navigate the dynamic landscape of YouTube. By applying the lessons learned from top creators and adapting them to your unique style, you have the opportunity to craft compelling content that resonates deeply with your audience. Embrace the journey of experimentation and learning, staying attuned to the pulse of your community and the ever-evolving trends. Remember, success on YouTube is a continuous evolution—a blend of creativity, analytics, and genuine connection. As you move forward, may your passion drive you, your insights inspire you, and your dedication propel you toward achieving your goals.

www.ingramcontent.com/pod-product-compliance
Lightning Source LLC
Chambersburg PA
CBHW071912210526
45479CB00002B/391